India

A CONCISE HISTORY

India
A CONCISE HISTORY

FRANCIS WATSON

Revised and updated edition
with a new chapter by DILIP HIRO

188 illustrations
4 maps

Thames & Hudson

Published in paperback in the United States of America
in 1979 by Thames & Hudson Inc. 500 Fifth Avenue,
New York, New York 10110

thamesandhudsonusa.com

Revised edition 2002

Library of Congress Catalog Card Number 2001099693

ISBN 0-500-28373-7

Printed and bound in Singapore by C. S. Graphics

Contents

Prefatory note   *page* 7

ONE   *Introduction*   11
UNITY AND DIVERSITY

TWO   *The Roots*   21
MEN AND CITIES ⁄ THE COMING OF THE
ARYANS ⁄ GODS, KINGS AND SAGES

THREE   *The Light of Asia*   39
THE POWER OF IDEAS ⁄ THE RISE OF
MAGADHA ⁄ ALEXANDER ON THE INDUS ⁄
THE MAURYAN EMPIRE

FOUR   *The Heirs of Ashoka*   53
INDO⁄GREEKS AND SCYTHIANS ⁄ THE
KUSHAN PRELUDE ⁄ THE IMPERIAL GUPTAS ⁄
HARSHA OF KANAUJ

FIVE   *The Deccan and the South*   71
THE TRADE FACTOR ⁄ THE ANDHRA
SUPREMACY ⁄ REGIONAL CONFLICTS ⁄ THE
EXPANSIVE SOUTH ⁄ THE EMPIRE OF THE
CHOLAS

SIX   *The Impact of Islam*   87
ARABS AND GHAZNAVIDS ⁄ THE FEUDAL SCENE
IN THE NORTH ⁄ THE TURCO⁄AFGHAN
PARAMOUNTCY

SEVEN *Moghuls and Europeans* 105

CHRISTIANS AND SPICES · THE FIRST FOUR
MOGHULS · THE NEW ARRIVALS · AURANGZEB
AND THE BREAK-UP OF THE MOGHUL EMPIRE ·
THE ANGLO-FRENCH INVOLVEMENT

EIGHT *The British Period* 129

THE PATH TO PARAMOUNTCY · REFORM AND
REVOLT · THE VICTORIAN ZENITH · THE TIDE
OF NATIONALISM

NINE *The new India* 159

FREEDOM BY DIVISION · THE SHAPE OF
DEVELOPMENT · INDIA IN THE WORLD

Dilip Hiro

TEN *India after Nehru* 175

THE DYNASTIC SUCCESSION · INTO THE
TWENTY-FIRST CENTURY

Select Bibliography 186

List of Illustrations 191

Index 196

The transcription of Indian words and names in a work for the general English reader is a matter on which no two writers are likely to be fully agreed. I have concluded that diacritical marks are best avoided altogether for this purpose, and one result of this is that some readers will find *sh* where they may have expected *s* (Ashoka for Asoka). I have also found it simpler to use the spelling *brahman* throughout, as referring both to the abstraction and the caste, instead of introducing *brahmin* at the point where it became a familiar usage.

A number of place-names memorized by most of us in more or less corrupt anglicizations have since 1947 been understandably restored (e.g. Cawnpore to Khanpur). In such cases I have been encouraged by the distinguished precedent of Sir Mortimer Wheeler to follow my own inclinations, which do not extend to changing the Ganges to the Ganga but willingly adopt Mathura for the rather horrid Muttra. Of the three possible corrections of Benares I have preferred Banaras as the easiest for the conservative to accept.

F.W.

1 India and the neighbouring countries. Ancient sites, caves and temples are indicated by small capitals (as for Mamallapuram, on the south-eastern coast), battle-fields by crossed swords.

Note Based upon Survey of India map with the permission of the Surveyor General of India.
© Government of India copyright 1972.
The territorial waters of India extend into the sea to a distance of twelve nautical miles measured from the appropriate base line.

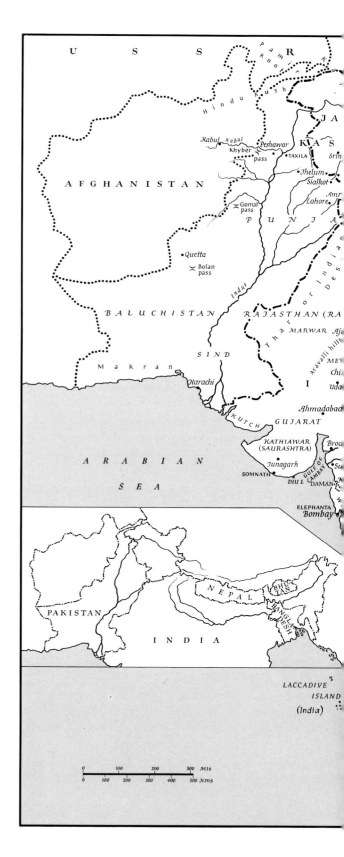

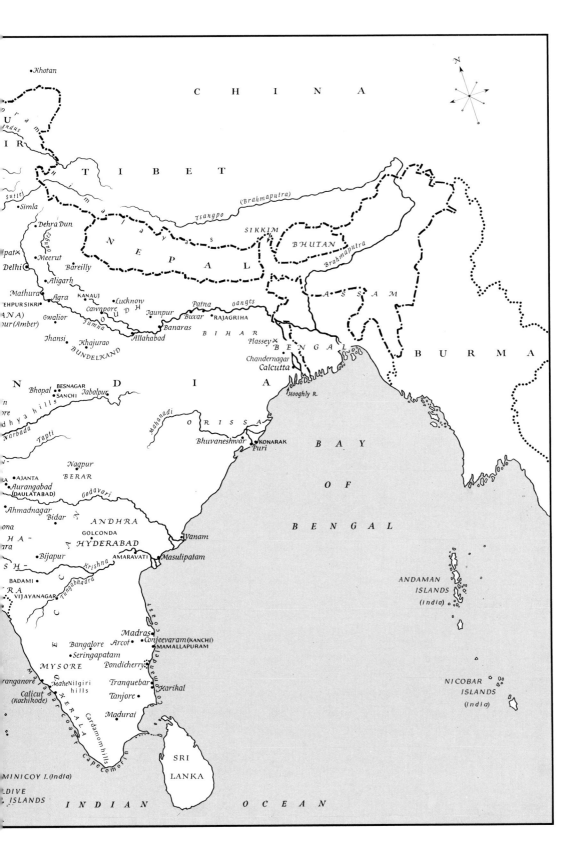

N

C H I N A

•Khotan

U
R
A
R

Indus

T I B E T

Sutlej

•Simla

Tsangpo (Brahmaputra)

•Dehra Dun

N
E
P
A
L

SIKKIM

B H U T A N

Brahmaputra

pat×

•Meerut

Bareilly

Delhi○

•Aligarh

A S S A M

•Mathura

Agra

KANAUJ

•Lucknow

Patna

Ganges

EHPUR SIKRI

Cawnpore

Jaunpur

Buxar

RAJAGRIHA

ANA)

Gwalior

Jumna

B I H A R

ur (Amber)

•Jhansi

•Khajurao

Allahabad

Banaras

Plassey×

B E N G A L

BUNDELKAND

B U R M A

Chandernagar

Calcutta

N

Bhopal

BESNAGAR

D

I

A

Jabalpur

•Hooghly R.

SANCHI

hya hills

Narbada

Tapti

Mahanadi

O R I S S A

Bhuvaneshvar

•KONARAK

B A Y

Puri

Nagpur

B E R A R

O F

AJANTA

Godavari

•Aurangabad
(DAULATABAD)

B E N G A L

Ahmadnagar

Bidar

A N D H R A

ona

GOLCONDA

HA -

HYDERABAD

Vanam

ra

Bijapur

AMARAVATI

Masulipatam

Krishna

ANDAMAN
ISLANDS
(India)

BADAMI

VIJAYANAGAR

R

A

Tungabhadra

Madras

Bangalore

Arcot

•Conjeevaram (KANCHI)

MAMALLAPURAM

Seringapatam

Pondicherry

NICOBAR
ISLANDS
(India)

MYSORE

ranganore

Mahe

Nilgiri
hills

Tranquebar

Karikal

Calicut
(Kozhikode)

Tanjore

•Madurai

Cardamom hills

SRI
LANKA

MINICOY I. (India)

LDIVE
ISLANDS

I N D I A N

O C E A N

CHAPTER ONE

Introduction

UNITY AND DIVERSITY

The Westernized name of India derived originally, through the Persians and the Greeks, from the region of the great river Indus (or Sindhu) which they knew. The application of the term to the entire peninsula was also external, compelling its extension, as the Indies, to the spice-islands which Columbus, seeking a circumnavigating route from Europe, thought he had reached in his Caribbean landfall. By retaining this name of India, the larger of the two independent dominions which were established in 1947 laid titular claim to the inheritance of an accumulated history. At that time it may have seemed paradoxical that most of the Indus basin went to form the new state of Pakistan. But the separation had precedents in the past, and could indeed be more clearly appreciated when in 1971 events precipitated, in Pakistan's geographically separated territory of East Bengal, the assertion of a deeply rooted regional identity against the political link of religious affinity (see pp. 175–6).

History is concerned with the greater concept for which geography provides a framework of essential simplicity. United or divided, India is in this sense the immense rhomboid, contained by the Himalayas that guard it on the north and the seas that meet at its southern tip, which begins to look small only when we view the whole Asian land-mass from which it depends. From the Pamir Knot and the complex of high ranges dominated by the Karakoram, the Himalayas curve eastwards for more than fifteen hundred miles like a gigantic curtain-swag to the junction of Upper Assam with China and Burma. Isolation is too strong a word for the effect of this magnificent wall, for its few and immensely high passes have always been penetrable by hardy pack-traders and by pilgrims to the hidden sources of Northern India's life-giving rivers. But as a deterrent to conquest it has played its part from earliest times to the Chinese invasion and withdrawal of 1962. The eastern hill region of the Burma frontier, though allowing tribal incursions into Assam, was also an impediment to major movements, unchallenged until the Japanese conquest of Burma in 1942.

On the north-west side, however, where the barrier turns southwards from the angle-buttress of the Hindu Kush, its character is different. The belt of dry mountainous country that reaches to the shores of the Arabian Sea is pierced by passes through which, from the Aryan migrations of around 1500 BC and even earlier, historical change has flowed again and again into India, lapsing only with the arrival of the

2 Opposite: the Sarnath lion-capital (there is a fourth lion at the back) adopted as India's national emblem. It was carved for the Mauryan Emperor Ashoka in the third century BC.

Moghul empire-builders, three thousand years after the Aryan tribes, on the threshold of a new era of European sea power. The Khyber, most famous of these passes, has been an immemorial trade-link with Central Asian and Mediterranean communications. South of the Khyber the main routes from the Iranian plateau are by the Gomal and the Bolan passes, and finally along the Makran coast.

From an early but uncertain period, raiders or settlers who reached the Indus river-system from the west and north-west were thereafter faced by the Indian Desert (Thar), and by the Aravalli hills, reaching north-wards from Gujarat to end in the low ridge by the Jumna river where Delhi now stands. These combined features forced them time after time into a relatively narrow neck of entry – the consequent field of decisive battles – from the Indus basin into the vast alluvial plain of the Ganges and its tributaries, of which the Jumna is the greatest. The Ganges plain, some 300,000 square miles of flat and fertile country, is the once-forested *Aryavarta* (home of the Aryans), the site of early empires, and the Hindustan of later history. Though separated from the Indus system, it merges in the myriad waterways of Bengal with that of the Brahmaputra, which flows for nearly a thousand miles through southern Tibet before cutting southwards through the gorges of the eastern Himalayas to reach the delta.

3 Himalayan peaks, home of India's ancient gods and guardians of her northern wall.

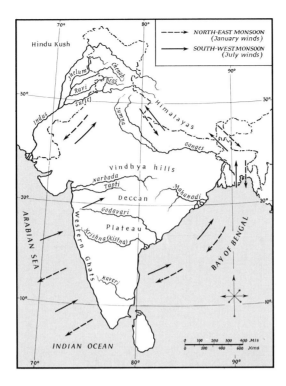

4 Winter monsoon winds, blowing from the north-east over land, are generally dry. The south-west summer monsoon, blowing from the ocean, brings 90 per cent of India's crucially variable rainfall.

Note Based upon Survey of India map with the permission of the Surveyor General of India.
© Government of India copyright 1971.
The territorial waters of India extend into the sea to a distance of twelve nautical miles measured from the appropriate base line.

5 Below: field-patterns of the highly cultivated Middle Ganges plain.

6 Rain-clouds gathering over the Kaveri. This and other Deccan rivers, unlike the snow-fed streams of the North, are fed only by the monsoon.

South of this distinct Gangetic region the land rises towards the geologically ancient Deccan, the peninsular South Land that confronted the Aryan immigrants with trackless jungle and unsubdued tribes. The line of historic demarcation is commonly called the Vindhya, sometimes the Satpura line, from the two ranges between which the Narbada runs westward to the Gulf of Cambay. The Deccan rivers, the Godavari, the Krishna (Kistna) and its tributary the Tungabadra, take the opposite course. Rising in the rugged chain of the Western Ghats, that for six hundred miles edge the Deccan plateau and precipitate the rainfall of a narrow coastal strip along the Arabian Sea, they find their way eastwards into the Bay of Bengal. As a cultural region of non-Aryan languages, South India has been broadly said to begin at the Tungabhadra river, but the Deccan uplands are continued southwards as a narrowing feature by the Nilgiri and Cardamom hills – through which, however, an important gap enabled Roman traders, for example, to cross eastwards from the Malabar to the Coromandel coast without having to round the southern extremity of Cape Comorin.

The large island of Ceylon, though it echoes an Indian relationship in reverting (in 1972) to the Sanskrit form of its name, Sri Lanka, has a separate history, and during its modern period of British rule (1815–1947) it was not part of the Indian dominion of Company or Crown but a colonial territory. Burma, which was annexed to British India in

14

three distinct stages between 1826 and 1886, was administratively detached by the India Act of 1935, and opted for independence outside the Commonwealth in 1947.

Geography and history have combined to produce the human diversity which strikes every visitor to India, though the much-quoted multiplicity of its languages comes to him only as a statistic, divided into five or six linguistic 'families' and swollen by the great number and variety of tongues and dialects surviving in regions, such as the extreme north-east, where natural obstacles have preserved isolated communities. An underlying theme of unity has been generally recognized by historians in the exceptional continuity of the religious tradition of Hinduism and its powers of assimilation, but few can assess with confidence the part played by fundamental beliefs and attitudes in the historical process. The influence of India's unique development of the hereditary caste system is a controversial as well as a complex study; but it may fairly be deduced that the services of this institution in the preservation of Hindu society were rendered at the expense of the wider development of a national consciousness. The localized cohesion remarked in the seventh century AD by the Chinese pilgrim Hsuan-tsang (see p. 67) in his Indian travels ('the people call their country by different names, according to the district') was still a challenge to the patriotic eloquence of Jawaharlal Nehru in the 1930s, as he relates in the course of his own *Discovery of India*.

7 Southern spice-lands, later planted with tea and coffee. A landscape in the Cardamom hills.

8 Humped bull, a specifically Indian breed from remote antiquity: impression of a Mohenjo-Daro seal, *c.* 2400 B C.

THE INDIAN BULL: symbol of continuity

9 Bull-capital from an Ashokan pillar in Bihar, third century B C.

10 Left: colossal statue of Nandi, the bull of the god Shiva, on Chamundi hill, Mysore.

11 Zodiacal bull on a gold coin of the Moghul Emperor Jahangir, *c.* 1620.

A principle of political unity, in the sense of dominion extended to India's geographical limits, had in fact been expressed at a very early stage in the idea of the *chakravartin*, or universal monarch. Such dominion, with the exception of the extreme unconquered South, was achieved at three separate periods: in the third century BC, by the Mauryan Empire culminating in the reign of Ashoka, in the fourteenth century AD, by the Turko-Afghan Tughluk sultanate, and at the end of the seventeenth century by the Moghul Aurangzeb. Each time, the consummation of empire preluded disintegration; and only the British, in a radically different process conditioned by maritime power and by rivalry with the French, found themselves masters of the peninsula to its southern tip. The unity which they went on to impose – while leaving a fragmented two-fifths of India in the limited control of its native rulers – was an administrative unity, made possible by unprecedented advances in communications. But beyond that it was the ground in which the Western concept of the nation-state was implanted through the English language.

English was not the first foreign tongue to be imposed on India as the language of government. In that capacity it replaced the official Persian, used by the British themselves until 1835, of an earlier conquest (see p. 139); but as the medium of higher education, and with the new facility of the printed word and of intercommunication, it promoted what its progenitors had foretold: the demand by a middle-class intelligentsia for democratic institutions on the Western model. The problem of satisfying these aspirations, after allowing for a simple reluctance to surrender imperial power, had a genuine basis in India's ethnic, linguistic, religious and social diversity.

12 The traditional sanctity of cattle as the foundation of India's agricultural economy allows bulls to roam at will in a modern city street – in this case Calcutta.

The unique character of this problem was patiently explained in the 1880s by Sir J. R. Seeley. In a series of lectures entitled *The Expansion of England* he stressed that India was not a nation in the sense understood by his Victorian audiences; its 'conquest', such as it was, had been accomplished by armies which were four-fifths Indian in their composition. 'There *was* no India, and therefore, properly speaking, no foreigner.' The sense of nationhood that was stirring, at the time that Seeley was speaking, among an English-educated minority in India, was perhaps too limited to be perceived. But the discovery of past glories which, then and later, so largely inspired it, was the product of Western scholarship: and primarily of the British, who had embarked upon the process a century earlier, in their first exercise of 'country power' in Bengal. The pioneering Sanskrit studies initiated by Warren Hastings, the first governor-general, had the practical aim of elucidating Hindu customary law, but his civilized tastes welcomed their extension, and the first result was a translation by C. H. Wilkins of the great philosophical poem, the *Bhagavad-Gita*. The brilliant scholar Sir William Jones, who followed with Kalidasa's classic drama, *Sakuntala*, was already a master of many languages when he arrived in Calcutta in 1783 as a judge of the Supreme Court. The work of a handful of scholarly civil servants, of whom Jones was the chief, paved the way for the philological recognition of the common Aryan origin of the main languages of Europe and Northern India, and the critical respect paid in the West to Sanskrit and its ancient literature encouraged the Hindu reforming spirit as well as a sense of inherited stature.

The task of bringing definition to Indian antiquity had begun in almost complete darkness, with Alexander the Great's penetration to the Indus in 326 B C as the only datable event (see pp. 45–7). Before the Arabic and Persian chronicles of the great Moghuls, and of the Muslim

13 Colonel Colin Mackenzie (1754–1821), first surveyor-general of India, with his assistants.

sultans who preceded them, history did not exist. In the abundance of Sanskrit learning, poetry and speculation there was no apparent place for it (though Kalhana's twelfth-century history of Kashmir is often cited as an exception). The very name of Ashoka, the greatest of India's ancient rulers, had been forgotten, his inscriptions unread until in 1838 James Prinsep, an official of the Calcutta Mint, found the key that unlocked the Brahmi and Kharoshthi scripts and, from recovered coinage, much of the ancient chronology (see p. 55). A few years later the labours of Brian Hodgson, the British Resident in Nepal, in the unexplored labyrinth of Buddhist literature (and his generosity with his manuscript collections) enabled the French scholar Eugène Burnouf to publish in 1844 his *Introduction à l'histoire du buddhisme indien*. From the latter part of the century generations of learned Indians extended and continued the work of historical revelation, in numismatics, epigraphy, documentary discovery and interpretation.

A similar story could be told of archaeology, for which the first important collections of material were made for the East India Company in South India, from about 1783, in the course of revenue surveying. Financial stringency having interrupted the work so well begun by soldiers and civilians like Colin Mackenzie in the south, Alexander Cunningham in the north, and James Burgess in the west, Lord Curzon's zealous reorganization of the department in 1902 bore remarkable fruit twenty years later, when excavation was begun under Sir John Marshall at the two main Indus valley sites of a hitherto unknown civilization dating back to the third millennium BC (see pp. 23 ff). This discovery, of which the traces had been recognized by a Bengali assistant, R. D. Banerji, gave a new and striking perspective to the patriotic view of the Indian heritage. At the same time, however, it upset the cherished primacy of the Aryan and Vedic contribution.

14 James Prinsep in consultation with learned Indians. He died in 1840, worn out at forty-one, after uncovering many centuries of lost history.

CHAPTER TWO

The Roots

MEN AND CITIES

Nowhere does the term 'Neolithic Revolution', with its suggestion of a sudden and spontaneous emergence of communities based on agriculture, seem less apt than in India, where hunters and gatherers even now survive in the remoteness of hill and forest. It is within living memory that the Baigas of Central India have been painfully compelled by authority to abandon shifting cultivation (burning of forest strips and sowing of seeds in the fertilizing ashes) and to move from axe-and-hoe agriculture to the plough, traditionally tabooed as a wounder of Mother Earth. Most of the two million Gonds retain their primitive ways, even though their tribal chiefs were assimilated many centuries ago into the feudal aristocracy. In the frontier hills of the north-east the age-old resistance to the encroachments of a more advanced society presented independent India with a serious problem when it adopted the political form of the Naga and Mizo demands for autonomy. One of the groups to attract anthropological interest, the purely pastoral Todas, light-skinned and patriarchally bearded, have dwindled to an aloof remnant in the Nilgiri hills of South India. Bombay, a city only three centuries old, gave the world the word 'coolie' by employing in casual labour the aboriginal Kolis, forest-dwellers and coastal fishermen, one of whom is recorded to have returned to a bow-and-arrow existence after travelling as far as Rome in service with India's World War II forces.

These and other such groups, to a total of some 30 million people in a population of 600 million, are the earliest and most rightful of Indians, as those who seek to protect them tirelessly point out. They are also living material for the study of the past, and have helped ethnologists to move from purely linguistic categories such as Dravidian (covering the non-Hindi languages of the South) towards racial classification of the pre-Aryan stocks. A Negrito strain, now very thinly represented, is held to be the oldest. This was succeeded and partly absorbed by the so-called Proto-Australoids, the genetic family relating some of the tribes of Central and South India to the Veddas of Ceylon and to the Australian aborigines. The third element, the Mongoloid, is almost confined to the north-eastern fringes; and the fourth, a Mediterranean type, had been added to the picture long before the Aryan incursions.

In the linguistic map there appears, in the now arid highlands of Baluchistan, an isolated pocket representing a language – Brahui – of Dravidian origin. Here, and in the neighbouring tracts of the western Indus plain and the Makran coastal strip, better climatic conditions in

15 Opposite: Nagas of the north-eastern hill-tracts at a village assembly. Former headhunters, this virile people helped to resist Japanese encroachment in the Second World War, struggled for autonomy thereafter, and have now been accorded a Nagaland State in the Indian Union.

the fourth millennium BC began to support the earliest settled communities known in India: an abundance of small villages similar to the Bronze Age settlements in Iran but distinctive in their several cultures. From about 3000 BC, however, in about a hundred sites so far uncovered, over a huge area of the Indus plain – almost a thousand miles from north to south – the pottery styles show a startling uniformity. The semi-isolated settlements had been succeeded by something very different: a homogeneous realm of villages and townships, with the river as the axis of communication, and with an agricultural surplus sufficient to support two capital cities, more than 350 miles apart: Mohenjo-Daro in the south, Harappa in the north.

Standardization, an ordered society, and ten centuries of relatively stable conditions, are among the surprising features revealed by excavation of these two urban centres. Both made use of vast quantities of baked bricks, presupposing the existence of forests to provide firing fuel. The ground-plans of both were not only similar, but retained through successive phases of rebuilding (see p. 31) a common principle, with a raised citadel, or acropolis, on the west, main streets laid out in grid-iron fashion, a network of lanes within each block, the better houses concealed in courtyards, and in both cities a clearly defined labourers' quarter. The great size of the granaries indicates a strong centralized authority, and the water-supply and drainage systems were extremely thorough. 'No Indian city', writes Dr Kosambi, 'possessed anything of the sort until modern times; far too many still lack these amenities.'

16 Opposite, left: a Koli from the Bombay area, where these tribesmen have become coastal fishermen and labourers.

17 Opposite, right: a Gond villager making fire. Many of this widespread tribe of the east-central region became culturally advanced and provided historic dynasties.

18 Opposite, below: a group of the diminished Todas, pastoral and polyandrous, photographed in the 1890s outside their beehive huts in the Nilgiri hills.

19 Megalithic tombs sketched in 1850 in the Deccan, where a Stone-Age culture had continued into the first century AD.

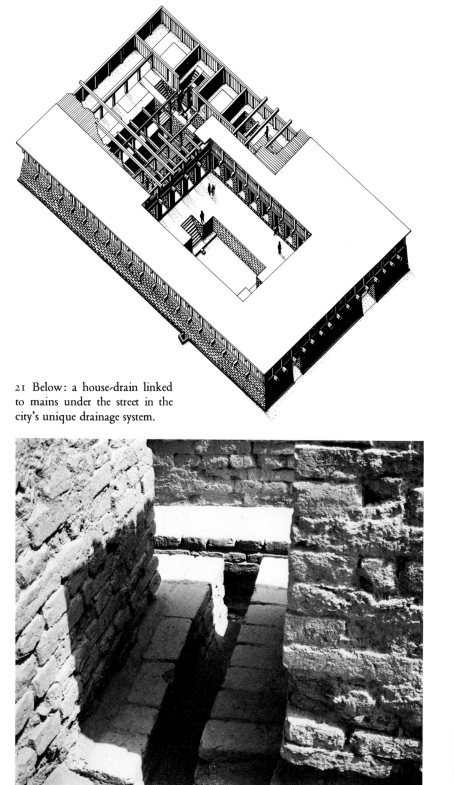

21 Below: a house-drain linked to mains under the street in the city's unique drainage system.

20, 22 The great bath (39 by 23 feet) drawn in reconstruction (opposite) with ancillary buildings, and as excavated (below) on the citadel, which is crowned by a Buddhist stupa more than two thousand years later in date.

23 Right: map of the Indus valley, showing the northern (Harappa) and southern (Mohenjo-Daro) centres, the more recently excavated Chanhu-Daro, and other sites of the third millennium B C.

24 Far right: Mohenjo-Daro seals depicting a 'unicorn', a rhinoceros, and a horned deity, possibly anticipating Shiva.

25 Opposite, left: necklace and ornaments in gold and semi-precious stones, from Harappa.

26 Opposite, right: decorated pot from Harappa, with leaf and bird motifs found throughout the Indus culture.

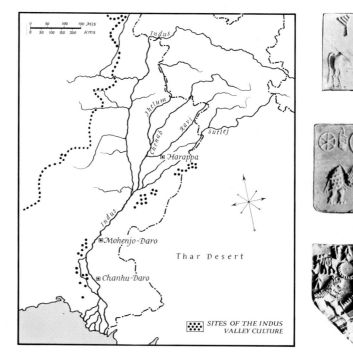

SITES OF THE INDUS VALLEY CULTURE

This civic sophistication sets the Indus civilization apart from its great contemporaries in Sumer and Akkad and Middle Kingdom Egypt. Its written language, which might dispel some of the mystery, remains undeciphered, and has survived only in brief seal-inscriptions apparently concerned with property or commerce. There seem to be no religious dedications, no names of rulers, and so far no dynastic tombs to shed light on a hierarchical system. The terracotta seals, of a type distinct from the Sumerian, are at once enigmatic and suggestive in the frequently consummate quality of their engraved images and in the subjects depicted, which include animals such as the elephant, tiger, rhinoceros and the Indian humped and dewlapped bull – as well as mythical beasts, emblems and figures. A horned deity depicted on some of the seals, seated in yogic posture, with erect phallus and accompanied by wild animals, has been seen as an early prototype of the Hindu god Shiva (see p. 33). The numerous small clay figurines of an earth-goddess, primitive by contrast with the seal-engravings, point to a popular fertility-cult; but the absence of monuments, religious or secular, is singular.

At Mohenjo-Daro the enormous stone bath on the citadel mound is presumed to have served ritual ablutions. Other evidence, such as the long conservation of a static pattern of life, has been used to support the argument for a dominant priesthood. All that we really know is that existence at this remote period must have been comfortable for an élite and was certainly highly organized. Humped cattle and buffaloes, goats, sheep and pigs, the camel and the elephant had all been domesticated, though not the horse (which has always, for some reason, presented breeding difficulties in India). The dog, first trained by

Paleolithic hunters, left his urban traces at the Indus site of Chanhu-Daro, in footprints chasing those of a cat across the once wet surface of some brickwork. The domestic fowl, one of India's gifts to the world, had by this time been tamed from the jungle-fowl.

Another distinctive Indian product, cotton, was already in use for clothing, as well as wool. Barley and wheat were the chief food crops, and both meat and fish were eaten. Iron was as yet unknown. Copper (probably from Rajasthan east of the Indus) was extensively used for household implements, though some of them were still of stone. Upper-class luxury and advanced craftsmanship were displayed in adorn-ments of gold and silver, ivory, jade, agate, crystal, lapis lazuli and other fine materials; and the absence of large works of art by which to dis-tinguish the Indus culture is compensated, not only by the best of the seals, but by a number of small sculptures – a bronze dancing-girl, a male torso, heads in steatite, and others – each of which has won high admiration in our own day.

There is enough that is unique and indigenous about Harappa and Mohenjo-Daro to leave the question of influence from or upon the Sumerian culture an open one. Of a flourishing trade between the two there is firm evidence, both by land across the Iranian plateau and by sea from a port near the mouth of the Indus. Hugging the dangerous coastline to reach the Persian Gulf, Indian crews used a 'compass-bird' – a crow which would fly when released towards the nearest point of land. The story that was later included in the Buddhist *Jatakas* of traders to Babylon using this device – exactly as recorded of Noah in the Bible and of Gilgamesh in the Sumerian epic – is pictorially confirmed on one of the Mesopotamian seals.

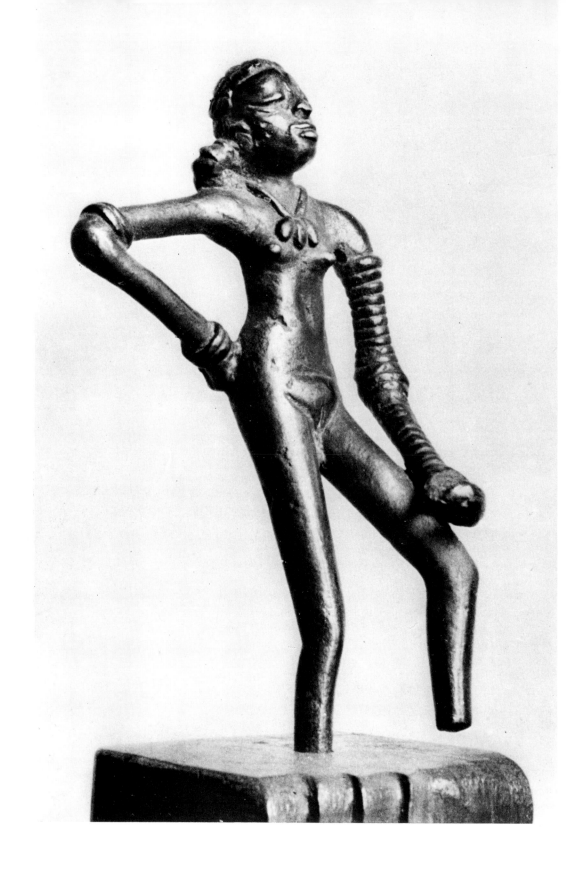

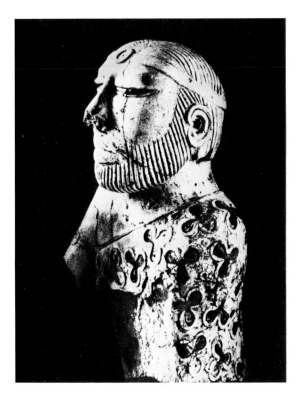

27 Opposite: bronze figurine, $4\frac{1}{2}$ inches high, assumed to be of a dancer, perhaps a slave, from Mohenjo-Daro. The facial type has been suggested as Dravidian.

28 Left: steatite bust of a man, $29\frac{1}{2}$ inches high, from Mohenjo-Daro. The trefoil pattern of the shawl, repeated in other Indus finds, may indicate Sumerian connections.

29 Below: bronze goat, $2\frac{3}{16}$ inches long, from Mohenjo-Daro, and carved terracotta monkey, $2\frac{3}{8}$ inches high, from Harappa.

ART OF THE INDUS CULTURE

Recent excavations have shown the Indus civilization to have been wider in its extent and influence than was previously supposed; and the uniformity of the evidence over an immense area has prompted Sir Mortimer Wheeler to infer 'something like an imperial status . . . the vastest political experiment before the Roman Empire'. Its mysterious obliteration is thereby rendered all the more intriguing. However the people of the Indus cities met their doom, the Aryans who succeeded them were barbarians in comparison, though their self-given name meant 'noble' or 'free-born'.

THE COMING OF THE ARYANS

From early in the second millennium B C the urban cultures of Western Asia were increasingly threatened by that recurrent instrument of history, the hardy nomads of the grasslands of Central Asia. In the words of the Mesopotamian chroniclers, 'their onslaught was like a hurricane: a people who had never known a city.' The tribes who brought their Aryan languages and their Aryan gods to Iran and India, while a separate wave flowed westwards into Europe, may not have been the sole executioners of the Indus civilization. Mohenjo-Daro in particular provides evidence of trouble and decay over several centuries before 1500 B C, the date now roughly agreed for the first Aryan immigrations through the passes of the Hindu Kush. But the same site also illustrates, with a huddle of skeletons, the final drama of an overwhelmed defence. There is also, in the collection of Sanskrit hymns called *Rig-Veda*, the earliest product of the Vedic tradition from which, in default of material remains, our knowledge of the next millennium has somehow to be gleaned. Renowned for the beauty of its invocations to the creative spirit of the natural world, this tradition is at the same time positive in the pride of conquest and the concept of racial and religious superiority.

The *Rig-Veda* was not at first committed to writing, but memorized (see p. 32). Almost a quarter of its hymns are addressed to the rain-god Indra, not simply as the seasonal banisher of drought but as the great storm-warrior and wielder of the thunderbolt. Irresistible in strength, gargantuan in appetite, fair-complexioned and bursting with rude vigour, Indra often calls to mind the deified hero of some Norse or Celtic myth. From details of his exploits the horse-drawn chariot of the Aryans, holding a charioteer and a warrior, can be reconstructed as a prime factor of conquest in the plains. The horse, praised in splendid verses in the *Rig-Veda*, must have been as terrifying a novelty to the foe as it was to prove in the Spanish conquest of the Incas in the sixteenth century, but there is little evidence of its use independently of the chariot: effective cavalry had to wait the curiously late invention of the stirrup. 'Destroyer of Citadels' is one of Indra's epithets, and in the Land of the Seven Rivers (later to be reduced by desiccation to the five which gave the Punjab its name) he assisted an Aryan chief by tearing to pieces 'like old clothes' the defending forces of a place called Hariyupiya – surely Harappa? In his capacity as 'Releaser of Waters', moreover, Indra is praised for feats suggesting the destruction of the dams now known to have been in use for flood control and irrigation in the basin of the Indus, which by shifting its course had caused Mohenjo-Daro to be rebuilt several times. 'On circumstantial evidence', to quote Wheeler again, 'Indra stands accused.'

The Sanskrit vocabulary is rich in pejorative terms for the appearance, customs and character of the various peoples encountered by the invaders, whether as enemies in pitched battle, peasant communities overrun, cattle-raiders, refugees from defended cities, or wild forest-hunters. Often they were 'noseless' or flat-faced demons, and always they were 'godless' in their unseemly ways and their indifference to the Aryan pantheon, its rites and sacrifices. From the post-Vedic epics and *Puranas* (miscellaneous sacred texts) such fanciful opprobrium as the description of one-legged aborigines who shaded themselves with a single enormous foot found its way many centuries later, through Pliny and other classical writers, into the travel-lore of medieval Europe.

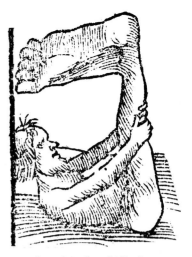

30 The Sciopodas of Pliny's *Natural History*, pictured in Europe among India's wonders as late as 1544.

The generalized name of *dasas*, which began by meaning 'enemies' and came to mean 'subjects', at all times carried the signification of a darker-skinned race. It would be an over-simplification to suppose that the descendants of the Aryans are found today in the northern half of India and in the higher castes, and the indigenous (Dravidian) strain in the South, in the lower castes and among the tribes. But the persistence of a social prejudice in favour of a light (in matrimonial advertisements 'wheaten') complexion cannot be overlooked. In this connection it is often pointed out that the word *varna*, as applied to the four-class system recognized from Vedic times, means 'colour' ('caste' comes from the Portuguese and was not used before the sixteenth century). These four classes were of priests (*brahmans*), warriors (*kshatriyas*), peasant farmers (*vaishyas*) and serfs (*shudras*), and in theory the subjugated elements could be admitted into the Aryan system only at the lowest level (see p. 36). The religious sanction for a strict maintenance of the four divisions, however, is either a late Vedic text or, as some think, a subsequent interpolation at a period when miscegenation had gone so far as to threaten the whole system. There is a note almost of desperation in the invocation which lays one more task upon the mighty Indra: 'O Indra, find out who is an Aryan and who is a Dasa, and separate them!'

Behind the advancing warriors, agricultural settlement accompanied and gradually gained over pastoral nomadism, in which wealth was at first entirely in cattle. Herds of oxen, sheep and goats gave the Aryans meat (taboos against beef or other flesh were not yet in operation), milk products, and wool for their few garments. The knowledge of cotton cultivation had vanished for the time being with the civilization of their predecessors, but barley and possibly wheat were grown at the first stage of settlement. *Soma*, the unidentified and sanctified potion used in ritual, was one of several intoxicants. Women appear to have had a respected status, and there is no reference to child-marriage. Games, dancing and chariot-races are mentioned in the early Vedas, which also include the lament of an unsuccessful gambler. Musical instruments were developed, and jewellery of some kind came to be worn by the more

31

31 A brahman priest, wearing the sacred thread of his caste, reading from a palm-leaf manuscript. For many centuries the scriptures were preserved by oral tradition alone.

important Aryans, but no art-objects have survived for comparison either with those found in the Indus culture or with the admired 'animal style' produced by the nomads of the Euro-Asian steppes. Their absence might be partly attributed to the burning of their dead by the Indo-Aryans, but simple burial was also practised.

The ways of these vigorous clans and families pushing in from the north-west differed totally from those that had characterized the long-established cities of the Indus valley. In this sense, as has been said, the newcomers were barbarians. But they were not primitive. They had no written language because they needed none, but the feat of memorizing and handing down an increasing body of oral 'literature' has to be borne in mind as we peruse it for clues to their life and thought. After the loss of the characters used by the Indus civilization (see p. 26) there is no evidence of a script until about the fourth century B C, a thousand years later, though some use of writing must be presumed from perhaps a couple of centuries earlier. As spoken tongues the sacred and elaborate Sanskrit and the 'natural' vernaculars, generally called Prakrit and reflecting a degree of Aryan mingling with the indigenous peoples, existed side by side. Even after Sanskrit was fully mature, however, the priestly ban on the committal of the religious texts to writing was effective for many centuries. The oldest *known* manuscript of the *Rig-Veda* dates from the fifteenth century A D – nearly three thousand years after the assumed time of its composition – but the Vedic hymns are used today at Hindu wedding ceremonies, in an astonishing example of continuous tradition.

The gods of the immigrant surge were elemental rather than territorial. Next in importance to Indra was Agni, the god of fire. The presiding sky-god Dyauspitar (in whom the Anglo-German scholar Max Müller recognized, in a flash of philological insight, Zeus, Jupiter and the Old Norse war-god Tyr) was fading to decline when the Aryans entered India. A secondary or rival Indra was found in Rudra, commanding a band of divine warriors called Maruts. The sun-god Surya and the dawn-goddess Usha are addressed in Vedic hymns of great beauty. Yama, the god of death, was seen as the first man, like Adam. A few hymns to Varuna, as a prime mover of the universe, foreshadow the abstraction of Brahma, later to claim some kind of embodiment in the brahman priests. The Hindu triad of Brahma, Vishnu and Shiva was not formulated until the Vedic pantheon had been penetrated by popular cults; and the belief in successive incarnations (*avatars*) of the godhead, with Rama, Krishna and eventually the Buddha himself numbered among the avatars of Vishnu, could only follow the acceptance of a concept of metempsychosis (transmigration) which does not appear until the later Vedas, and then as little more than a hint.

Among the deities that superseded the Vedic nature-pantheon, Shiva probably emerged from the cults scattered by the fall of the Indus cities.

32, 33 Post-Vedic deities. The four-headed Brahma (left) embodied the idea of primal creation, but was little worshipped, while Shiva (right), his rival in many myths, was accorded a powerful cult in his various aspects, beneficent as well as destructive. Both figures are from South India, tenth to eleventh century AD.

34 The elephant-headed Ganesha: a South Indian bronze probably made in the tenth century AD, when this god began to be generally propitiated for fortune in any project, and accorded a popular annual festival.

35 Above, right: bronze figure of Hanuman, long-tailed monkey-messenger and faithful servant of Rama in the *Ramayana*, given semi-divine status for his selflessness. The tools of the sub-caste that paid for this eleventh- or twelfth-century image are shown at the base.

The elephant-headed Ganesha and the monkey-god Hanuman may once have been tribal totems. Most intriguing as to ancestry is the widely appealing figure of Krishna, the inspiration in later times of so much poetry and art, the focus of devotion in so many aspects. The vast accretion of Krishna-legend was a protracted process, drawing upon multiple sources, and frequently revealing the efforts of Brahmanical orthodoxy to combat the pervasive influence of a humanized rural deity more ancient than the gods of the Vedic sacrifices. This dark hero of a dark-skinned people, divine herdsman and lover of the milkmaids, had his earliest cult in Central and South India, and in one distinctive episode is represented as fighting, and winning, a battle against Indra, the deified champion of the fair-skinned invaders. In his eventual form as an *avatar* it can be promised that whenever he is needed in the struggle of good with evil, Krishna will come again.

The main vehicle for the Krishna-legends, and for the epic myths of India's beginnings, is the *Mahabharata*, expanded over many generations into the world's longest poem. Together with the shorter *Ramayana* – traditionally assigned to the sage Valmiki – the *Mahabharata* embodies the later folk-memories and reinterpretations of tribal events which, in so far as they have any historical connection, belong to several centuries from about 1000 BC. The fluctuating conflict in which the Pandavas finally overcame the Kauravas – the central theme of the *Mahabharata* – can be geographically placed in the strategic *doab* (two rivers area) of the upper Ganges and the Jumna. The region of original settlement in the Punjab had been lost to sight in the late Vedic texts, and the eastward expansion, possibly motivated by the pressure of new arrivals from the north-west, involved internecine fighting between Aryan tribes now organized into petty kingdoms. The primeval forests of the Ganges plain had only just begun to yield to the tillage which afterwards swept them away, but in the clearances villages developed comparatively quickly into fortified settlements imposing enough to reveal to archaeologists a distinct Ganges civilization of the first millennium BC. Indraprastha on the Jumna (subsequently the first site of Delhi), the now excavated Kaurava capital of Hastinaputra to the north of it, and further down the Ganges the mighty Kaushambi and the earliest foundation at Varanasi (Banaras), are examples of a late Vedic and post-Vedic development which was doubtless stimulated by the introduction of iron-working. The use of iron in supplementation of copper was vital to the jungle clearance of the eastward advance. It also added to the possession of land that of ores as providing causes of conflict and the weapons for waging it.

The originally localized civil feud of the *Mahabharata* came to be exaggerated by later additions into a legendary subjugation of the entire Indian peninsula, with the non-Aryan forest-dwellers generalized as *nagas*, or 'serpent-people', having their own dynasties. In the *Ramayana*, which is presumably later since the action begins lower down the Gangetic plain, the exploits of a virtuous and deified ruler (Rama) were given a specifically sub-continental setting: a Trojan war with an Indian Helen (Sita) carried off by the demon king (Ravana) of Ceylon (Lanka). The foundation for this post-dated romance, which for generations of popular audiences has happily blurred the boundaries of history, religion and myth, must be sought in whatever southward penetrations, from about 800 BC, the developing society in the north was able to make. The Vedas themselves do not look further south than the Vindhya hills.

The clan conflicts for land and power which the epic tradition glorifies had produced by the sixth century BC a profusion of northern states in which sixteen can be distinguished as of main importance, from Gandhara in the extreme north-west to Magadha and Anga along the lower Ganges, in what afterwards became Bihar and Bengal. Meanwhile, in the wake of this expansion from the original *Aryavarta* (see p. 12), the rise of the Achaemenid power in Persia (Iran) produced new incursions from the north-west. Under Cyrus (558–528 BC), Gandhara was added to the Persian Empire as a much-prized satrapy (it was at that time an important source of gold), and under his successor, Darius, power was temporarily extended across the Indus. Semitic influence, working through the Persian contact, has been found in the reintroduction to India of a written language, and the Gandharan capital of Taxila soon entered upon its great reputation as an intellectual centre. Around 500 BC Atreya, a famous name in early botany and medicine, was teaching at Taxila, which at a somewhat later but uncertain date also produced Panini, the revered grammarian of Sanskrit.

Even on a purely oral basis education, as an exclusive reserve of the brahman priesthood, could become highly systematized. The adoption

36 Scene from the *Ramayana*, longest and most popular of epics, in a Hindu temple-hanging.

of a script had other compulsions in a society which was by now evolving a commercial sector, requiring weights and measures (one of the notable standardizations of the vanished Indus culture), coinage, and all that goes with possession, taxation and administration. Keeping pace with these developments, the first modifications had appeared in the four-class pattern of society (see p. 31). The growing mercantile class came to occupy the third category as vaishyas, displacing the cultivators into the lower order of shudras, and thus introducing below them the casteless group that was to harden into 'untouchables'.

The relationship of chief significance, however, was that between the brahmans and the kshatriyas. The emergence of politically organized states from the chaos of tribal land-wars took two distinct forms. Side by side with kingdoms such as Kosala and Magadha there existed republics – or more properly oligarchies – in which the tribal tradition of a representative assembly was retained in a corporate form of government. Decisions were taken, in debatable cases by majority vote, by a council which met periodically in the chief town; and these decisions were executed by appointed officials. The presiding official in the assembly carried the title of *raja* (from the same Indo-European root as the Latin *rex*). The title was not hereditary in states of this kind, but its holder and his peers of the governing body were normally land-owning kshatriyas, who at this time were often mentioned above the brahmans in the hierarchical pattern.

Several instances can be traced of republics becoming kingdoms, and vice versa; but the monarchical system, and with it the orthodoxies of caste, tended to supervene in the larger states, in which tribal loyalties were inevitably weakened. Here the influence of the brahmans, through the rituals which gave sovereignty its political and popular authority, and the state itself a magical support, was less liable to erosion.

In the later portions of the *Rig-Veda*, and most notably in the famous 'Hymn to Creation', there is already discernible that strain of sceptical inquiry into the cosmic essence which was to fructify in the several distinct systems of Hindu philosophy and to preserve, at the still centre of a priest-ridden, myriad-godded vortex, the continually renewed inspiration which dissolves creeds and systems, merging the transcendent with the immanent and the universal with the particular. A supreme expression of this profound search can be recognized in the *Upanishads*, the first of which are assigned to 600 B C, at the end of the Vedic age, but may have been somewhat earlier. Within the Vedic millennium, so bare of the material marks of man's passage, his spiritual quest had proceeded from the robust infancy of polytheistic animism to the subtlest reaches of conceptual thought. Some two thousand years later a Mohammedan prince, hearing of the *Upanishads* in Kashmir, had fifty of them translated into Persian, from which the Frenchman Duperron eventually rendered them into Latin, to become for Schopenhauer in the nineteenth century 'a consolation in life and a reconciliation with death'.

The earliest bards of the Vedic revelation had held a special place in the Aryan imagination as ancestral sages, neither gods nor priests but *rishis* (hence *Maharishi*, 'great sage'), more powerful than either. The unknown composers of the *Upanishads* were distinguished from their fellow men as detached, contemplative 'forest teachers', unconcerned with sacerdotal establishments or with popular magic. The same process introduced the figure of the *yogi* or ascetic – paralleled throughout the world by the self-abnegating solitaries of other cultures, but uniquely Indian in its unbroken continuity, and in the acceptance of techniques for mystical experience as the proper pursuit of full-time, lifelong devotees. The Greeks, whose curiosity was stimulated by reports of India's philosophers of forest and cave, called them 'Gymnosophists' in allusion to their nakedness.

Whether at the purely meditative level of a dispassionate search for truth, or at that of fantastic controls and mortifications of the flesh for the acquisition of occult powers, or in the lower and often charlatan regions of folk-magic, the yogic ideal fell outside the Brahmanical canon and had somehow to be absorbed. This was assisted by the formal recognition of four stages of man's life, of which the first could fitly be spent as the pupil of a forest teacher and the last, after two stages of worldly preoccupation, as a period of preparation for death, again with the benefit of specialized guidance and example. With the countenance finally given to the cult of Shiva, whose austerities in his ascetic aspect were the means of upholding the cosmos, the primary Vedic motive for the priestly sacrifices became an anachronism. But before this happened the early *Upanishads* had been, as it were, legitimized as an extension of the Vedic liturgical texts called *Brahmanas*. The culminating Upanishadic utterance, and probably the Hindu text most universally prized today, is the *Bhagavad-Gita* (Song Celestial), put largely into the mouth of Krishna and interpolated in the *Mahabharata*.

37 A king taking counsel with *rishis* (forest-sages), from a sixteenth-century copy of one of the eighteen puranas, non-Vedic pseudo-historical scriptures compiled from the sixth century AD onwards.

CHAPTER THREE

The Light of Asia

THE POWER OF IDEAS

Material advances in the Ganges basin favoured the rise of the early kingdoms. The republics, formed singly or in confederations by clans such as the Panchalas, the Mallas and the Videhas, grew up to the north of the river-line, reaching into the Himalayan foothills. This was the region that gave birth to the two great reformers, Gautama the Buddha and the Jain Mahavira. Both were of kshatriya origin; and both, by their indifference to class distinctions and their rejection of sacrifices as a means to salvation, undermined the status of the brahmans. They were contemporaries in the late sixth and early fifth centuries B C. Their appearance followed by about a century the flowering in Iran of the influential cult of Zoroaster, whose followers much later provided the Parsi ('Persian') refugee founders of a small but important Indian community.

The procession of world-teachers through these two centuries can be followed from Lao-tzu and Confucius in China through the Hebrew prophets to the Greek philosophical schools of Pythagoras and of Socrates. In the Indian context the evident ferment of thought – with the Buddhist and Jain teachings emerging from other reforming experiments – was tinged with pessimism. Relatively rapid changes in social organization, outgrowing the theological framework, may well have produced anxiety about the human condition; and the powerful idea of transmigration, with its corollary of causality (*karma*) operating upon successive incarnations, had not long taken hold of men's minds when the Buddha was inspired to see endless rebirth as an intolerable chain of suffering which the spirit of man must break by freeing itself from earthly cravings.

The message of Mahavira was also concerned with the escape from rebirth, though from different premises and with a greater emphasis on personal austerity. Both approaches introduced monastic institutions to Indian society, although Mahavira (who claimed to be expounding doctrines originating some 250 years earlier) may have found small existing hermit communities to build upon. Born about 540 B C in what is now Bihar, he became a wandering ascetic at the age of thirty, and after his enlightenment preached in the Ganges valley until his death (allegedly by self-starvation) at the age of seventy-two. His materialist doctrines spread to the south, and then to the west. At inter-vals they gained favour as a guide to statecraft, but the most significant following was found in the mercantile sector – partly because Jain rules

38 Opposite: ferocity yields to the Buddha. At the left in this railing-roundel from the Amara-vati stupa, a mad elephant sent to kill him wreaks destruction, but at the right bows at his feet.

39 Prince Siddhartha, afterwards the Buddha, going to school in a chariot drawn by oxen. His companions carry lesson-tablets and ink-pots.

of non-possession were at first confined to landed property. The Buddhist injunction against killing was extended by the Jains to the whole animal kingdom (including insects), thus virtually excluding cultivators as well as soldiers from the fold. After surviving brahman reassertion, Muslim invasions and its own schisms, Jainism numbers today upwards of two million adherents, mostly in Gujarat.

By a different destiny, Buddhism was to lose altogether the commanding position that it came to hold in the land of its origin, and yet to become a world religion. The birth of its founder, on an estate near the present India-Nepal border, has been dated either 566 or 563 BC. Gautama was his patronymic, Siddhartha his own name, and he was the son of a leading landowner near the city of Kapilavastu in the Himalayan foothills. The legends that were to provide signs and wonders for his birth, and a wealth of stories for his previous incarnations, promoted

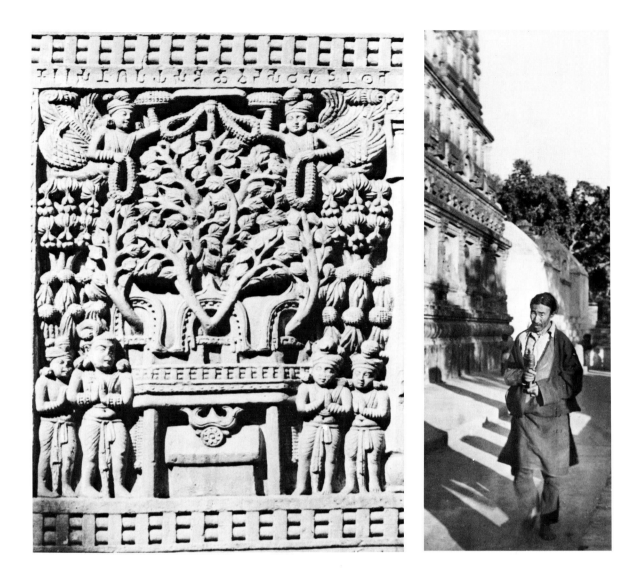

him also, by way of emphasis on his Great Renunciation, to princely rank and the palatial luxury of a later age. But the sheltered upbringing, the shock of discovering outside his home the facts of human pain and anxiety and death, the abandonment of a young wife and child in order to seek a solution to human suffering, and the vain consultations with brahmans and ascetics, ring true through all embellishments of the famous story. The victory of his Enlightenment under a pipal-tree is commemorated at Bodh-Gaya, 150 miles east of Banaras, to which he then made his way to deliver, at near-by Sarnath, the 'Sermon in the Deer-Park', compressing for a handful of his disciples the essence of his new teaching. For the remaining forty years of his long life he preached extensively in the villages and towns of the Ganges valley. Wherever he went he founded *viharas* (rainy-season refuges) or *sanghas* (permanent communities) of monks, and occasionally of nuns.

40, 41 The tree under which the Buddha attained Enlightenment, adored as the sacred Bodhi-tree on a gateway pillar at Sanchi (left), has been continuously commemorated at its site at Bodh-Gaya, Bihar, by a temple which attracts many pilgrims: here a Tibetan is seen circumambulating the shrine with his prayer-wheel (above).

41

42 Hindu divinities paying homage to the Buddha, symbolized by the throned Wheel of the Law, on a relief from Mathura of the second century B C.

Outside the monastery they were missionary friars, sustained by whatever food the poor could spare and forbidden (at first) to accept money offerings.

The strength of Gautama's Middle Way lay in the human breadth of its appeal. Steering between the extremes of worldliness and asceticism, it offered by the Eightfold Path of ethical living and thinking a means of salvation to all – monk or layman, king or peasant, man or woman, without the aid of priests or even, for those who could dispense with them, of gods. It did not, however, directly challenge the prevailing tradition, and the elevation of the Buddha himself as an object of veneration was a later development, beginning in the third century B C with symbolic representations and producing a figurative image only at the beginning of the Christian era. His relics, however, were distributed after his death and enclosed in the plain reliquary structures called *stupas* – basically a dome surmounted by a spire – which multi-

43 The sixth-century stupa at Sarnath, near Banaras (165 feet high
but unfinished), where the Buddha set forth his teaching in the
'Sermon in the Deer-Park'.

plied thereafter as the characteristic monuments of the spreading teaching. Although the first acceptance of this teaching may naturally have
come from the kshatriyas of the Buddha's own class, brahmans were
soon numbered among its adherents. The indirect nature of the sub-
version of Brahmanism (for example, in the objection to blood sacrifices) helps to account for the absence of any evidence of serious brahman opposition in the formative stages. Reaction was postponed over
many centuries of the Buddhist advance to a status recognized by
powerful rulers, materially assisted by the support of the merchant class,
and underpinned by assimilating polytheistic myths and folklore.

In the area of his own preaching on earth, Gautama's impact was
attested by the gift of monastic lands and groves from the propertied
sector. Shortly after his death it was at Rajagriha (Rajgir), at that time
the capital of the Magadha kingdom, that the first Great Council was
held (483 BC) for the compilation of the doctrine and the monastic

code, both of which became subjects of dispute and heresy in later centuries. And the language of the first Buddhist texts, which in the Ceylon canon was afterwards to be known as Pali, has been identified as an idiom or dialect probably spoken in Magadha.

THE RISE OF MAGADHA

The Buddha's contemporary on the throne of Magadha was Bimbisara, an energetic despot favourably regarded in the Buddhist chronicles, although he did not dispense with the conventionally enormous blood sacrifices required for sovereignty. His capital at Rajagriha, its cyclopean defences picturesquely sited among seven hills, was on the edge of the iron-rich area that sustained the rise of Magadha power, and he introduced the novelty of a standing army, paid out of the taxation of a politically organized territory. This enabled him to annex his eastern neighbour of Anga, gaining the prospect of trade access to the Ganges delta and the sea.

The obscure birth of this Magadhan king – the first to kindle the idea of universal (meaning North Indian) monarchy – is a reminder that hereditary rulers, though normally of kshatriya origin, were drawn in various instances from all the four main divisions of society. Bimbisara's position and that of his realm were further strengthened by dynastic marriages (he was credited with five hundred wives). When he died in 490 BC – starved to death in captivity, it was darkly said, by his son and successor Ajatasatru – Magadha's only powerful rival was the Kaushala kingdom on the west, astride the central Ganges valley.

Kaushala commanded also the more difficult trade tracks to the south, into the Deccan. Under Ajatasatru Magadha gained the upper hand over Kaushala, and extended this southward commerce. Hides and cloth are mentioned among northern trade items, while 'conch-shells, diamonds, precious stones, pearls and gold are available in plenty in the south'. The evidence comes from the *Arthashastra* (Science of Material Gain), the classic and remarkably Machiavellian treatise on statecraft which embodies, under the later but undated authorship of the brahman Kautilya, theories of state expansion and authoritarian government which had been successfully tried out by the brahman advisers of Ajatasatru. The espionage and deceptive stratagems by which the northern fringe of republics and tribal societies were softened up before military action, as well as the Magadhan take-over of Kaushala when its king and army were conveniently overwhelmed in a cloudburst, were in the correct technique of the *Arthashastra*. But the careful procedures which Kautilya was to recommend for the recurrent crises of succession were not followed, or not effective, when Ajata-satru's son, around 413 BC, lost the throne of his forebears to the still mysterious dynasty known to tradition as the Nine Nandas.

It is to Chandragupta Maurya, the first of a more powerful line, that Kautilya is commonly attached as a brahman *éminence grise*; and Chandragupta's initial manœuvres with the advancing Greeks in the Punjab bring us to what is sometimes called the first undisputed date in India's history, that of Alexander the Great's invasion in 326 BC.

44

Alexander's raid, as many Indian and Western historians prefer to call it, was certainly less immediate in its consequences than a conquering invasion: for the drama of the young Macedonian's progress through the tottering Persian Empire was halted at that empire's furthest reach on the line of the Indus, and his death at Babylon on the return postponed for another 150 years the period of Hellenistic supremacy in north-west India.

The Persian satrapies of Gandhara and the Indus had in fact reverted to the rule of Indian chieftains shortly before the Alexandrian enterprise. Two centuries of the Persian connection had provided a significant bridge between East and West, bearing trade, ideas and language as well as the weight of impossible legend obscuring the sounder information – such as the revived use of cotton – gathered in the fifth century BC by Herodotus. Indians and Greeks had both been subjects of the great empire. A valued contingent of Indian bowmen had fought under Xerxes. 'They must have marched', wrote Rawlinson, 'through the bloody defiles of Thermopylae.' And the annihilating thoroughness of Alexander's operations against the wild mountaineers of the Hindu Kush had more in it than the flanking protection of his main advance. It was meant, said the young conqueror, to punish Indian participation in the Persian project of enslaving Athens.

44, 45 A defile in the Hindu Kush, on the route into India taken by Alexander the Great, and Alexander portrayed on a silver tetradrachm.

46 The Indian King Porus on his war-elephant, attacked by Alexander on horseback: a coin struck by Alexander to celebrate his victory in 326 BC.

Had the drive into India, however, been carried to its intended conclusion at the dimly envisaged eastern seaboard, Alexander would have adopted his colonizing tactics of accommodation with the indigenous rulers and peoples under a Greek paramountcy. He had begun by summoning the chiefs and kings of the Indus region to meet him near the present Kabul, and the city of Taxila received him with open arms. The Indian ruler who subsequently forced him to battle near the flooded Jhelum was known to the Greeks as Porus, and had collected from a confederation of local princes a huge army of infantry, cavalry and elephants. Superior tactics and the discipline of the Macedonian phalanx, which stampeded the elephants, brought the Greeks a hard-won victory. But it left them with admiration for their opponents, and Porus became Alexander's friend and ally. It was then that the army that had marched and fought from the Mediterranean decided that it had had enough. The world conqueror, leaving the provinces he had won and the settlements he had founded in the charge of Greek generals and Indian associates, turned southwards to meet his fleet at the mouth of the Indus and thence westwards, with a part of his forces, through what had now become the forbidding desert of the Makran.

That was the last that India saw of Alexander, and his name is not mentioned in its chronicles of the time. There is a tradition, however, supported by Greek writers, that before he left the Punjab he had been approached by Chandragupta Maurya and vainly urged to move eastwards against the kingdom of Magadha, which was still ruled by the Nanda dynasty. Chandragupta's opportunity was to come, as it turned out, in the period of uncertainty and disturbance after the with-drawal of the Greek army. Within a year of Alexander's death (323 BC) Chandragupta had not only exploited revolts in the north-west to displace Porus from Taxila and master the region of the upper Indus and its tributaries, but had defeated and killed the last Nanda and succeeded to the coveted throne of Magadha itself – to which he may have had a partial claim by birth.

Which of these startling achievements came first is not clear, but it would seem likely that the well-organized Magadhan army was used for the north-western operation, rather than the other way round. Some eighteen years later, when Alexander's former general Seleucus Nikator, the legatee of his Asian conquests, advanced to the mountain marches, he was either repulsed or discouraged by the Mauryan strength. Chandragupta gained further Afghani and Baluchi territory to round off his possession of Gandhara, and reportedly a daughter of Seleucus in marriage. The Macedonian, according to Plutarch, got a present of five hundred war-elephants.

THE MAURYAN EMPIRE

It was an Indian, not a Greek empire, that reached, by the end of the fourth century BC, from the Hindu Kush to the Bay of Bengal. Its capital had been moved from hilly Rajagriha to riverside Pataliputra (the modern Patna in Bihar), a great city of which the Greek ambas-sador Megasthenes left a lively though fragmentarily preserved account. Its houses of two and three storeys were mainly built of wood and un-burned brick, and there were strict precautions against fire. The im-perial palace was also timber-built, magnificently plated and decorated (by Persian craftsmen, as some have surmised), and set among gardens and aviaries. Besides a defensive wall, twenty-five miles in length and with 570 towers, the city was protected on two sides by the Ganges and a tributary, and on the other two by a broad and deep connecting moat, used also for drainage.

The whole of the ambassador's journey from the Mauryan frontier to the capital – a good twelve hundred miles as the crow flies – was made by a road well supplied with milestones and direction posts and contin-uing (he was told) beyond Pataliputra to the Ganges mouth. Inspired, perhaps, by the Royal Road of Achaemenid Persia, this must have been a valuable trade artery as well as a strategic communication for the Mauryan Empire, which maintained an enormous army. Under Chandragupta and his son Bindusura (though they did not, as Plu-tarch had it, 'subdue all India') power was pushed southwards, thrust-ing in some form as far as the Mysore plateau. To be productive on this scale, military force required the organization of an elaborately authori-tarian state.

The *Arthashastra* (see p. 44), though strictly a theoretical treatise, appears to expand the observations of the Mauryan system made by Megasthenes in the capital. The Greek was mistaken in supposing that there was no slavery, which was an acknowledged institution, though not in the form familiar to the Mediterranean world. And

47, 48 The elaborate luxury of
the Mauryan court at Pataliputra
is expressed by feminine fashion
in a terracotta figurine (right).
Below: a chariot-wheel uncovered
during excavations at Pataliputra.

though his tribute to the high moral tone of urban society is not to be brushed aside, it must be qualified by his own evidence of the severity of the laws, which included death for, among other offences, defrauding the revenue or killing an elephant (not a sacred beast but a capital asset). His account of the protection found necessary for the monarch is also eloquent. Chandragupta, it seems, was closely guarded in his palace, never slept twice in the same bed, had all his food tasted in his presence, and only appeared in public, heavily escorted, on certain magnificent occasions of festival.

The ambassador's portrayal of a highly organized civil and military administration is carried further by the *Arthashastra*, where the entire system is that of a police-state, supported by an army of spies, *agents provocateurs* and secret assassins. Its cool self-justification is found in the material progress of an empire in which land clearance, the mining industries, and a significant proportion of the agricultural economy, were state monopolies, and a close control was also attempted over the advancing commercial classes.

On these remarkable foundations the great Emperor Ashoka (*c.* 273–232 BC), second in succession from Chandragupta, built something of a different quality. The edicts carved for Ashoka, with a clearly permanent intent, upon imperishable rock, the inscriptions

49 Rock at Girnar, in Gujarat, inscribed with Ashokan edicts in the third century BC, sketched by Lieutenant Thomas Postans for James Prinsep in 1838. The Emperor's inscriptions have been found as far west as Kandahar.

upon the pillars of inimitably polished sandstone which he set up throughout his vast dominions, yield a new concept of kingship and indeed of the nature of man. Even when the *Arthashastra's* robust avoidance of cant has been conceded, its cynicism is rebuked in the contemplation of the Ashokan model: an equitable society in which the function of absolutism is translated by the ruler as 'the debt that I owe to all living creatures'.

During his first few years as emperor, Ashoka, who had previously served as governor in two secondary capitals, Taxila and Ujjain, maintained the methods of his predecessors and exerted himself to round off their legacy of an empire stretching from sea to sea, and from Kashmir to the southern Deccan, somewhat north of the present alignment of Madras and Bangalore. All that was required was the final and hard-fought subjection of the Kalingas (occupying today's Orissa on the Bay of Bengal). And it was this operation which provoked what one of his inscriptions described as 'His Sacred Majesty's remorse . . . because the conquest of a country hitherto unsubdued involves the slaughter, death and carrying away captive of the people.' The 'Law of Piety' which he thereupon adopted, and inculcated in the three or four peaceful decades remaining to his reign, was a public acceptance of the message preached two centuries before by the Buddha – whose name, however, was nowhere mentioned in the inscriptions.

The postulate of a moral political economy, substituting for violent suppression a practical assault on poverty and insecurity, is one of the early features of the Buddhist canon, not implausibly ascribed to Gautama himself. Ashoka's public works – the provision of free hospitals and veterinary clinics, bathing-tanks, wells and drinking-places for cattle, shade trees and rest-houses for road travellers – were acts of social compassion without respect to quick returns. His revulsion from warfare, in an empire freed for the time from internal threats, reduced an extravagant army to a defence force concentrated where it might be needed, in the north-west. For the peace and settlement of his dominions, especially of the tribal areas, Ashoka introduced a new class of travelling supervisors (Kosambi translates them as 'High Commissioners of Equity') responsible for examining and redressing complaints on a basis of regard for the needs and customs of particular groups and minorities. Caste was something about which none of the Maurya dynasty seemed rigid (Chandragupta is thought to have been of mixed origin), but the tyrannizing bureaucracy of the system had produced social tensions, and Ashoka's evident objective was the reconciliation of classes. He restored the neglected routine of administrative reports, which he was ready at all times to receive and study, and he required the higher civil servants to make quinquennial tours of the different regions. His own wide and frequent journeys helped to temper the centralization of a system in which the only appearance of the ruler in the countryside had been in war or the lavish pursuit of game.

Ashoka's abandonment of the royal tradition of the chase was in line with the reverence for animal life that he showed by a vegetarian table. To his subjects blood sacrifices were forbidden, but hunting was not, except of 'non-edible' beasts and birds on protected lists. Outside the imperial household beef and other meat was openly available: the cow was not then sacred.

Buddhism did not become a state religion – a concept foreign to Indian ideas, then as now; but the movement grew rapidly with the prestige of Ashoka's support, and became known beyond India with the Emperor's missionary-embassies to Seleucid Syria, Ptolemaic Egypt and other Hellenistic kingdoms, Ceylon (where he sent his own son) and probably Nepal. Several of the innumerable stupas set up in Ashoka's reign were regarded as his personal foundation, among them the inner brick core of the Great Stupa at Sanchi. The multiplying monasteries were self-governing institutions, protected and at intervals guided by the ruler, but mainly financed – now that the rule against cash offerings had lapsed – by the laity, rich and poor. The Jains (bitter rivals in the Buddhist chronicles) also enjoyed Ashoka's patronage, and he was on good terms with the brahman priesthood, with whom remained the ritual functions connected with birth, death, marriage and initiation which – like sacrifices – were rejected in the Buddha's doctrine.

Another religious group that flourished under the benign Emperor was the resolutely independent ascetic sect of the Ajivikas. The Barabar caves in Bihar, assigned to Ajivika use by Ashoka, are the earliest in the great succession of India's rock-cut architecture. Like the railings and gates at Sanchi (see p. 52) they imitate in stone the wooden structures which in Ashoka's reign began to be replaced also by free-standing buildings of stone. One of the fine commemorative columns, carved at this time, under evident Persian influence, bears on one of its capitals a group of four lions, today the emblem of the Republic of India (p. 10).

50 Opposite: an Ashokan edict-pillar, one of the few remaining perfectly intact, erected in 243 BC at an already ancient site at Lauriya Nandangarh, near the Nepal border. The shaft is a single piece of polished chunar sandstone, surmounted by a capital with a seated lion.

51 Entrance to the Lomas Rishi cave in the Barabar hills, near Gaya, patronized by Ashoka and providing the earliest rock-cut version of wooden buildings such as had existed from Vedic times.

CHAPTER FOUR

The Heirs of Ashoka

INDO-GREEKS AND SCYTHIANS

With the death of Ashoka in 232 BC the outlying provinces of his huge empire, beginning with Taxila, soon broke away. The Kalingas, whose subjection had caused him such remorse, revived their strength in the east; and from the coastal area south of them the Andhra king-dom, as it is usually called, began the expansion north-westwards across the Deccan which renewed the separation of the Aryan home-lands from the other world of South India. Within fifty years the last of the Mauryan line was assassinated in the sight of his army by his brahman commander-in-chief, under whose usurping Shunga dynasty – which itself survived for little more than a century – the elaborate ceremonies of the Great Horse Sacrifice were revived. These were the orthodox prerequisite for 'universal' kingship, but nothing could pre-vent dominion from shrinking back to the earlier confines of the Magadha state.

Beyond the Hindu Kush the Greek governor of Alexander's Bactrian colony had detached it from the Seleucid supremacy. Around 200 BC these Bactrian Greeks overcame the now weakened defences of Gandhara and the upper Indus in an invading movement which was extended, before very long, southwards from the Punjab to reach the Sind coast and the Saurashtra (later Kathiawar) peninsula. The fea-tures of some of their kings in India are known to us from their out-standingly fine gold and silver coinage, and the fame of the greatest of them, Menander, has been preserved by the Buddhist treatise surviving as *The Questions of Milinda*. Menander's capital (at the site now occupied by the Punjab city of Sialkot) is described in this work as well defended, beautifully laid out 'in delightful country', and a flourishing trade centre. Its streets, thronged with elephants, horses, carriages and pedes-trians, were said to 'resound with cries of welcome to teachers of every sort': and to these Menander, the philosopher-king, proved consist-ently superior in argument until the celebrated Buddhist monk Nagasena arrived in town with his disciples, 'lighting up the city with their yellow robes like lamps, and bringing down upon it the breezes from the heights where the sages dwell'. In public debate Nagasena converted the King to Buddhism, but Menander was not thereby deterred, as Ashoka had been, from further warfare. He moved down the northern plain with the aim of subduing what remained of Maga-dha, only to be recalled by Scythian pressure in his rear, and to die in battle.

52 Opposite: one of the four carved gateways of the railings with which the Great Stupa at Sanchi, begun by Ashoka and enlarged after his death, was em-bellished in the first century BC. The imitation in stone of previous timber structures is here manifest.

53 Menander, Bactrian Greek philosopher-king of north-west India (115–90 BC). The reverse of the coin shows Pallas Athene.

54 Bactrian silver dish with a war-elephant, possibly that of Eucratides, 167–159 B C.

55 Mounted warrior, from Sarnath, fifth century A D.

This Scythian wave of the Central Asian displacement had been checked by the Parthian Mithridates and diverted against the Bactrian homeland, from which it overflowed, with some Parthian admixture, into the Indo-Greek area from Gandhara as far as Mathura and Ujjain. First as Persian satraps and then as independent rulers, their prominence in India, where they were known as Shakas (Latin *Sacae*) is identified from about the middle of the first century B C. How far the Greeks (*Yavanas* in Sanskrit) had by then advanced is uncertain, but there is an account of a siege of Pataliputra, and evidence of Greek settlement and influence has been traced in Orissa.

The significance of the Indo-Greek encounter, though doubtless distorted in the first excitement of Western researches, goes well beyond the brief span – between 100 and 150 years – of Hellenistic rulers in Northern India. Megasthenes at the court of Chandragupta Maurya (about 306 B C) had been struck to find among the brahmans points of agreement with the Greek philosophers 'concerning generation, the nature of the soul, and many other subjects'. But although doctrines

56 A Parthian shooting at the gallop, first to third century A D. Parthians, of mixed Persian, Mongolian and Bactrian descent, played their part in the Indo-Hellenistic encounter and established a local dynasty at Taxila.

57 Below: a donor couple, in patrician costume, portrayed in stone at the entrance to the great chaitya cave at Karle (second century A D).

corresponding to the Indian concept of causality (*karma*) and phenomenal illusion (*maya*) can both be read in Plato's *Republic* (as also metempsychosis, which the Greeks claimed to derive from Egypt) there is nothing to prove the dominant direction, at this early stage, of a flow of ideas between Greece and India. Channels of communication existed, but it is only in the area of a known and continuous contact, which begins with the Bactrian kings, that signs of a working synthesis can be sought.

Aside from the Menander story, they are few but curious. The refined Greek coinage changes presently to a cruder mintage of Indian type, inscribed with the Brahmi and Kharoshthi characters which were to lead Prinsep, nineteen centuries later, to the decipherment of the Ashokan edicts (see p. 19). A lone surviving monument, the Garuda column found at Besnagar in Central India, is inscribed in Brahmi as the dedication of a Greek, Heliodorus, 'a worshipper of Vishnu and an inhabitant of Taxila'. In the area of the later Bombay the Karle and Nasik cave-sanctuaries record votive donations made by prosperous

Greeks. It is evident that many Hellenes settled freely and comfortably as citizens, adding their contribution to the ethnic pattern and taking their choice of Indian names and Indian tutelary deities. When the rulers of Bactrian descent disappeared from the record, the process of Indo-Greek cultural assimilation was to some extent continued by the Parthian element among their Shaka successors. In the Shaka period, also, a new strand enters the fabric. If the Apocryphal Acts of Thomas can be believed, the Evangelist came to India after the death of Jesus, and was hospitably received in cosmopolitan Taxila by the Indo-Parthian King Gondopharnes. It is a tradition that need not invalidate the more continuous one of St Thomas's mission to South India, and of the martyrdom commemorated in the famous shrine beside which, from the seventeenth century, the city of Madras grew up.

THE KUSHAN PRELUDE

A further phase of this age of invasions was inaugurated, early in the first century AD, by the Kushans, who had emerged from the Mongolian heartland as a rearward wave of the movement of nomads, had taken to settled ways in the Bactrian region, and now moved through the passes to supplant the remaining petty kingdoms of north-western India. The Shaka ruling class, however, survived the Kushan dynasty to found further principalities, known to history as the Western Satrapies. These lasted for another two and a half centuries.

The mark made by the Kushans is that of their only well-known ruler, the great Kanishka, whose headless but inscribed statue stands with the confidently planted feet of a conqueror, and wearing the garb of the steppelands. Kanishka's prosperous empire, though it reached south-eastwards down the Ganges as far as Banaras, was essentially a Central Asian power. On the west it came within six hundred miles of the Roman frontiers, and Kanishka sent an ambassador to Trajan. Northwards it pushed through Kashmir and beyond the formidable barrier of the Karakoram to take in Kashgar, Yarkand and Khotan on the oasis trade-route; and for a time to threaten the declining Han dynasty of China, whose pretensions Kanishka reflected by styling himself Son of Heaven.

Gandhara in the Kushan period was thus not a frontier province but the hub of an empire. Its position in the web of caravan routes between Asia and the Mediterranean brought material wealth and facilitated the flow of ideas. For Buddhism, of which Kanishka was a signal patron and probably a convert, the region provided a beacon to the non-Indian world – and literally so in the gigantic tower erected by Kanishka near his capital of Purushapura (Peshawar). It was still standing in AD 630, when the Chinese pilgrim Hsuan-tsang (see p. 67) described it as thirteen storeys high, with a superstructure of gilded copper discs. From the rubble which is all that now remains there has been rescued a gilded reliquary bearing Kanishka's name and figure and the name of his Greek or Indo-Greek master-mason. The near-by Buddhist monastery, endowed by Kanishka, became an important seat of learning; and the Kushan city of Sirsukh, the fourth and last to be built on the Taxila site, featured a Zoroastrian temple as well as a great range of separate buildings forming the Buddhist university of Taxila.

The Mahayana (Great Vehicle) form in which Buddhism, at the beginning of the Christian era, made its way through Central Asia into China was influenced by the other faiths with which it was in contact in this Kushan cosmopolis. Its doctrinal authority was evolved in six months of discussion by a council held under Kanishka's patronage in Kashmir, but boycotted by the Buddhist fraternity in Ceylon, which handed down the strictly purer Hinayana, or Lesser Vehicle, that was to predominate in Burma and Thailand. The Mahayana compromise with popular beliefs, for instance in finding room for a Buddhist pantheon and sainthood, assisted both its advance in India at this time and its extension through northern Asia. In the same development the Buddha figure in art replaced the various symbols by which alone he had hitherto been represented. In the eclectic style of Gandhara sculpture he is sometimes realized as an Aryan prince, but more often idealized as an

58 Opposite: model stupa from the Jaulian monastery, near Taxila, of the type from which the Far Eastern pagoda evolved.

59 Kanishka, in this inscribed life-size effigy from Mathura, scarcely needs his head to express his mastery of an empire extending from Central Asia to the middle Ganges.

60–62 Three of the great variety of facial types signalling the spread of Buddhism throughout Asia from the first century A D, when the Buddha's portrait began to replace or supplement his symbols: from Gandhara (right), Cambodia (below, left) and Thailand.

Olympian anthropomorphic god, with classical motifs of dress and architecture and attendant figures.

The art of Gandhara, at first accepted in the West as 'Hellenistic', and for that reason prized above India's wealth of medieval sculpture, is now seen in a different light: not as a legacy of Greek influence from the time of the Bactrian kings but rather as a cultural product of Kushan commerce with the Roman Empire. Its Hellenistic content is largely indirect among the styles and mannerisms absorbed from the Mediterranean world in the service of an Indian faith that dispersed the synthetic result along the trade-routes of Central Asia. The communications of the Kushan Empire, however, stretched back to its Indian confines; and here, most notably in the region of Mathura, the iconographic change probably preceded slightly that of Gandhara, and certainly took an entirely Indian form. An occasional hybrid element was borrowed from the north-west. But the serene spirituality of the Indian Buddha was developed independently, in the context of a sensuous tradition asserted in the triple curve of female bodies of a marvellous grace, and against a background of radiant kinship with the animal and vegetable world of field and forest.

Mathura was a rich and important city under the Kushans, trading to the west coast as well as through Gandhara. Examples of the fine Mathura ivories exported, with other Indian luxury crafts, by the latter route, have been found in a hoard of Syrian glass, small Roman sculptures, Chinese lacquer and other treasures, under the ruins of Kanishka's palace at Begram, now in Afghanistan. These may have been seizures for customs dues, buried when the city was sacked in the third century

63, 64 Sculpture from Mathura. The Buddha (above, left) is attended by a subservient Brahma. The guardian *yakshi* (above) is both forest-nymph and court-damsel.

59

AD at the hands of the rising Sassanid power of Iran. This marked the end of the Kushan dynasty (whose last representative took the Indian name, associated with Krishna, of Vasudeva). The history of the separate elements of Northern India is thereafter exceedingly obscure until the appearance of the imperial Guptas in AD 320.

In later Brahmanical texts the Kushans were dismissed as alien innovators, along with some ten centuries of *mlechcha* (barbarian) domination of various kinds. But the 'Golden Age' of the Guptas had had its prelude in the florescence over which Kanishka had presided. Literature as well as art had begun to evolve a classic form, and Sanskrit (in which Kanishka himself is said to have composed a long poem) to acquire its definitive role. The reputation of great Buddhist scholars, such as Asvagosha and Nagarjuna, is a Kushan legacy. Chanaka, the first luminary of Ayurvedic medicine, was Kanishka's physician.

THE IMPERIAL GUPTAS

The Gupta dynasty is taken to extend, though interrupted in the fifth century by Hun invasions, from 320 to about 540. As an era of great works of culture, such as the plays of Kalidasa (see p. 63) and the finest in the long series of Ajanta cave-paintings, it is stretched somewhat further. Aside from vainglorious royal inscriptions there is the testimony of the Chinese pilgrim Fa-hsien, who moved about India from 405 to 411.

65 Chandra Gupta I with his queen, on a gold coin of his reign.

Fa-hsien's tributes to a general state of content under good government are those of a devout Buddhist scholar travelling from monastery to monastery to study their system and collect and copy sacred texts. The improved position of the orthodox brahmans had been exemplified in the recourse by the Gupta rulers to the Great Horse Sacrifice to sanction their dominion. But Buddhists were among the advisers of all the Gupta monarchs, who moreover ignored caste principles and xenophobic sentiment by a policy of intermarriage with pre-Aryan clan families and the introduction of Kushan, Scythian and Greek women into their households. It seems to have been an alliance by marriage with the ancient and virile Lichchavi clan – which had just then renewed its importance by establishing a dynasty in Nepal – that paved

the way to the Magadha throne for the founder of the new state, Chandra Gupta I. (His name, and those of his successors, may be thus divided to avoid confusion with the Mauryan Chandragupta of more than six centuries earlier.)

Some of the Mauryan ideas of administration reappear under the Guptas. At its height in about 400 the Gupta Empire had expanded westwards from Magadha across the width of India, taking in the Western Satrapies and the lower Indus valley, but not Gandhara or Kashmir. In the northern mountain rim Kumaon, Nepal and Kama-rupa (northern Assam) are represented as paying tribute. Southwards, however, beyond the Vindhya divide and the Narbada river, there was no reconquest of Ashoka's dominions of the Deccan. According to the possibly biased inscriptions of Chandra Gupta's son Samudra, who was responsible for much of the expansion and adopted the title 'Exterminator of Kings', this was a matter of prudent magnanimity. The southern rulers against whom he had campaigned down the eastern edge of the Deccan were listed as having been defeated and captured but reinstated. In another category come the tribal 'kings of the forest country' whom Samudra Gupta 'made to be his servants'.

Where the Gupta control was direct, as in the Ganges valley, the Mauryan model was modified, leaving administrative and even some policy decisions to be taken at provincial and district level. The rural areas, increased by new agricultural settlements, were policed and protected by dispersed units which could all be summoned for war purposes if necessary. As in Mauryan times the state provided essential public works and also regulated trade. In municipal government, in which the guilds of artisans and craftsmen were represented, the pre-dominant interests were commercial.

Mercantile vigour was also reflected in the prosperity of Buddhist communities, and on a smaller scale of the Jains. Internally, as well as on the long and taxing land routes to China, Buddhist monks shared the journeys of merchants, with time enough to discuss the puzzles of the soul's existence and destiny. The great monastic complexes were often sited at centres of commerce; and the cave-monasteries, if more retired, were near enough to the trade-routes to be sure of supplies, donors and lay visitors. Buddhism had never signified isolation from the

66 Travel in the second century A D. Frieze of pilgrims on a stone lintel-beam from Mathura.

world, but its increasing association with the wealthy classes may have been one of the causes of its decline in India, since the Brahmanist challenge at this period can be seen in a pioneering penetration of the remoter countryside and the jungle, and the assimilation of rural cults and customs in the colourful fabric of Hindu religion. Though Mahayana Buddhism had done the same, it was in the end to lose ground as a message by the dilution of essential distinctions, such as the virtual atheism of the Noble Eightfold Path: whereas a Brahmanical system founded on sacrifice and ritual would eventually be strengthened by syncretism to the point where the Buddha could be reduced to one of the lesser avatars of Vishnu. In the intellectual climate of the Gupta period, however, the different sects and systems coexisted in their intellectual functions, and it was from their scholastic debates that the so-called six philosophies of India received their standard formulation. Primacy among the Buddhist universities now passed from Taxila – beyond the Gupta boundaries, and in the fifth century devastated by the Huns – to Nalanda, near the earliest Magadhan capital of Rajagriha, hallowed by the Buddha's own footprints.

67 Excavated monastery at Nalanda, one of the six that were combined under the Guptas into a renowned university. The divisions in the background are the foundations of the monks' cells.

From the first the Gupta rulers laid claim in their inscriptions to cultural achievement. Chandra Gupta II (385–414), who moved his capital to Ayodhya (Oudh) and completed the advance to the western coast, has been identified by one of his titles with the otherwise mythical king of that name whose court at Ujjain, which now regained its importance, was said to have been illuminated by the 'Nine Jewels' of literature. Chief among these was Kalidasa, author of the far-famed *Sakuntala* and two other known plays, and lyric poet of the equally acclaimed *Cloud Messenger*.

The plot of *Sakuntala* is drawn from the *Mahabharata* which, like the *Ramayana*, attained at this time its most approved Sanskrit recension. The ancient but non-Vedic *Puranas*, enshrining grotesque but authoritative myths, were also given shape. The erotic compendium of Vatsyayana's *Kama Sutra* cannot be later than the fourth century (it was evidently known to Kalidasa). Its illumination of the life and cultured leisure of a citizen (*nagarika*), if not the sole reason for today's world-wide circulation of the translated work, may well reflect the opulent and relaxed civilization considered in the Gupta period as an

68 Gupta relief of the fifth century showing a scene from the *Ramayana*, which received its definitive Sanskrit form at this period.

63

69 The iron pillar, 23 feet high and unrusted, inscribed to Chandra Gupta II (375–413), on its later site near Delhi. It has the same 'Persepolitan' lotus-bell finial as the Mauryan columns of seven centuries earlier (compare ill. 50).

attainable ideal. On Indian literature and painting the *Kama Sutra* exercised a prolonged influence.

The sculptural art remaining from this period, though it is misleading to isolate it by the Western term 'classical', includes large figures of a fully achieved aesthetic harmony and a perfection of anonymous craftsmanship in which the theme and purpose, whether Buddhist, Brahmanical or Jain, provide merely iconographical variations, and those not always obvious. In addition to superb stone-cutting, the proficiency of casting in bronze or copper was of a high order; and a metallurgical feat of a different kind, which would be remarkable at any place or time before the twentieth century, produced the famous pillar of pure, and therefore still unrusted, iron to be seen near the present city of Delhi. It was removed thither from the original site at which, according to its inscription, it commemorated the imperial reign of Chandra Gupta II.

70 The high peak of fifth-century Gupta art and metallurgy: over life-size bronze Buddha (7 feet 6 inches high) from Sultanganj in Bengal.

Mathematical studies, of very ancient origin in India, were providing in the fifth century the formulations – including the all-important numeral notation of nine digits and a zero – which eventually reached the Arabs (who called mathematics 'the Indian science') and through them were communicated to Western Europe to make discovery and invention possible. Greek geometry seems to have been unknown in India, where progress was made by the different intellectual approach of abstraction. Greek astronomy, however, was acknowledged by the great fifth-century mathematician and astronomer Aryabharta as a notably 'god-like gift' to have come from 'barbarians'. The ranging spirit of inquiry of the Gupta era, and its liberal progress in the arts and sciences, was rather strangely (to our notions) accompanied by San-skrit codifications such as that of the mysteriously evolved 'Laws of Manu', aimed at a tightening of the regulations of caste for the preserva-tion of brahman exclusiveness.

71 Hsuan-tsang returns in 645 to the Chinese (T'ang Dynasty) capital at Ch'ang-an, with pack-loads of Buddhist manuscripts gathered in fifteen years of scholarly travel in India.

HARSHA OF KANAUJ

The White Huns, or Ephthalites, or as the Indians called them Hunas, were barbarians in the sense most painful to settled societies. Their ethnic position among the Central Asian hordes is disputed, but not their destructive ferocity. While Attila's Huns streamed across Eastern Europe to attack Italy in the mid-fifth century, a southward wave over-whelmed the Sassanid Empire in Persia and the Kushan remnants of the Indian north-west. Skanda Gupta (455–70) is credited with a brave defence of his western frontiers in face of this irruption, but by about 500 a Hun chieftain was recorded as far south as Ujjain. Although the invaders are believed to have been broken and repelled thirty years later, by a romantically mysterious hero from Central India called Yasodharman, the Gupta Empire was already falling to pieces under the strain. The line survived in smaller kingships through the century of confusion which followed, and even beyond it. But the title to a revived paramountcy in Northern India was won by a rival and arrest-ing figure, and for no longer than his own reign.

This was Harsha Vardhana (605–47), who came from Thanesar, strategically placed at the entrance to the Ganges plain, and established the capital of his new and brief empire down-river at Kanauj. His father, a local chief, had fought off the Huns besides feuding with his neighbours. Harsha, succeeding at the age of sixteen, set forth to avenge some family outrage, and for the next six years of conquest 'the elephants were not unharnessed nor the soldiers unhelmeted'. The territories that he gained, grandiloquently called 'The Five Indies' in his title, approxi-

66

mated to those of the imperial Guptas, except that they never reached the Indus or the western seaboard. Coupled with the cutting of the land routes and the collapse of the Roman trade under the Hun onslaughts, this reduced the influx of foreign specie as compared with earlier times. Fa-hsien's picture of prosperity combined with light taxation under Gupta rule is nevertheless repeated, and in more detail, by Hsuan-tsang (see p. 15), who in the seventh century spent eight of his fifteen years of Indian travel within the dominions of Harsha. The accumulation of wealth in the royal treasury by conquest, and in the Buddhist monasteries by endowment, lent glitter to this last pre-feudal system. Under Harsha the revenue was (at least theoretically) divided four ways between the expenses of state, the pay of public servants, the reward of learning and the distribution of gifts. He earned a name for open-handed splendour, and made a point of paying (probably in kind) for the forced labour that he employed on public works.

An index of economic pressure, however, and a trend of future consequence, can be found in Harsha's policies of restricting cash payments to those earned by military service, and of making grants of state land not only in the tradition of gifts to brahmans but also in lieu of official salaries. His most interesting point of reference to the distant memory of Ashoka is in his return to the Buddhist Emperor's practice of almost continuous travel for inspection and the redressal of grievances – a mobile authority in place of the Gupta attempt to decentralize.

Ashokan pieties seem to be echoed in Harsha's attention to roadside rest-houses and dispensaries, his personal charities, and his efforts to

72 Hsuan-tsang, a portrait from the Tun-huang ('Thousand Buddhas') caves, Western Kansu, China.

soften judicial severities by the use of moral suasion and the sanctions of social opinion. His reported prohibitions of killing and the use of animal food, however, were certainly temporary or limited. Hsuan-tsang mentions fish, venison and mutton as additions to the produce of intensive cultivation, with rice as a staple crop in the east, wheat and sugar-cane in the west, and a great variety of fruit and vegetables. Caste taboos against beef, intoxicants, onions and garlic were observed to be in operation by the Chinese visitor, who also noted that butchers and scavengers were confined to mud-built quarters outside the cities and, when walking, to the left-hand side of the roads. Dancers and courtesans, highly regarded in their professions, were outside the pur-view of caste and to this extent free of the restrictions suffered by their sex. Despite the exaltation of women in art and literature, these restrictions were as severe in Brahmanical texts as the other social controls, though the fantastic savagery of some of the Laws of Manu (see p. 65) is quite unreliable in regard to practice. Harsha is represented as having shared his throne on a public occasion with the widowed sister whom he had rescued from voluntary self-immolation on her husband's pyre. The rite which was to become known to the West as 'suttee' (although *sati* in fact refers to the exemplary woman, not to the practice) had been known in Vedic times, but seems then to have been performed only symbolically. The actual sacrifice, which developed in a privileged kshatriya context and is first positively recorded in AD 510, remained as voluntary as the force of custom allowed until a decadent rigidity turned it into a crude act of social violence (see pp. 90, 138).

Harsha was fortunate in having (beyond his official panegyrist Barna) so respectable a foreign admirer as Hsuan-tsang, who had been a guest at the court of the Emperor's Assamese vassal and was unwilling-ly surrendered on demand. There are also, to substantiate Harsha's cultural image, three known and surviving Sanskrit dramas from his own hand. To his reign and patronage are commonly assigned the work of Susruta in medicine, of the Vaisesika school in physics, Brahmagupta's anticipation of a gravitational theory, and in mathe-matics the calculation, much more correct than that of the Greeks, of a value for π.

The Buddhist university of Nalanda, to which Harsha added a large new monastic building, had four thousand students in his day. His early attachment had been to the Hinayana orthodoxy (see p. 57), but the famous assembly which he summoned to Kanauj after listening to Hsuan-tsang's exposition of the Mahayana doctrines was for their investigation by 'all disciples of the various religious sects or schools, the *sramanas* [Buddhist monks], brahmans and heretics of the Five Indies.' Inaugurated with enormous state, the debates ended in a tri-umph for the Chinese 'Master of the Law' and the teachings he sup-ported, so that Harsha found it necessary to issue a stern warning against any attempt to injure him. A conspiracy against the royal person was also uncovered, and five hundred brahmans were arrested. Having pardoned all but the ringleaders, Harsha fell victim in 647 to a murder plot set going by a brahman minister and carried out by the army.

The rebel was defeated and killed by an invading force sent from Tibet at the instance of the Chinese Emperor, with whom Harsha had been on good terms. But there was no lawful heir to succeed at Kanauj, which before long was under attack by the rival Palas of Bengal. Of the Pala dynasty the most noteworthy fact is the shelter which it gave in Bengal to a late development of Buddhism which, since it was permeated with magical rites and Tantric practices, has been regarded as debased. It was from Bengal and in this form that Buddhism during the next century was carried into Tibet, where it mingled with Mongolian adaptations of the Mahayana vehicle to form a specialized theocracy. As to Kanauj, Harsha's capital, the best tribute to the impact of his brief regime is that this city was to remain for several centuries the symbolic magnet for the ambitions of warring chieftains in Northern India.

73 'Suttee', the rite in which the *sati* sacrificed herself on her husband's funeral pyre, was known in Harsha's empire. As a voluntary privilege it was afterwards idealized in many famous examples, especially among the Rajputs. This drawing was made some years before its suppression in 1829.

CHAPTER FIVE

The Deccan and the South

THE TRADE FACTOR

Recoverable history has thus far occupied the Indian scene with the tumults and achievements of the North. Only for the Mauryan century (c. 340–240 BC) have we seen empire effectively extended southwards of the Vindhya line; and after Ashoka had marked its limits on the Mysore plateau with his rock-edicts, the megalithic culture with which it was there in contact continued to erect its characteristic monuments down to the first century AD, the beginning of Southern India's 'historical period'.

This does not mean that the apparently empty frame of southern prehistory can be filled by the traditional Aryan generalization of hostile primitives as diabolical in their ways as in their appearance. In the South a megalithic phase persisted in association with the advances based on metal cultures, and beside the burial-dolmens are found stone tanks and irrigation works. On the east and south-east of the Deccan uplands that were penetrated from the North for their mineral and forest products, broad areas of low-lying cultivation stretched to the long seaboard where an enterprising people, without the inhibitions of the land-hugging Aryan code to impede them from venturing upon 'the black water', earned the commercial reputation that was recorded by Greek and Latin authors at the beginning of the Christian era.

Before that the seaborne traffic with India stretches into conjectural antiquity, lit by flashes such as King Solomon's importation, in the tenth century BC, of ivory and apes and peacocks. From the eastern side, Indian voyages to Lower Burma and the Malay Peninsula in search of gold and tin are generally placed at least as far back as the sixth century BC – coevally, that is, with the Indian contacts of the advancing Persian Empire in the West. With the expansion of maritime trade in the first and second centuries AD the Indian Ocean takes on the aspect of a single area, with India in a central position of advantage, the Roman imperial economy a major factor, and Southern India a particular beneficiary. The Alexandrian Greek author of the *Periplus of the Erythrean Sea* contrasts at this epoch the forbidding Deccan jungle, swarming with wild beasts, with the thriving maritime centres export-ing pearls and shells, diamonds, sapphires, beryls and other precious stones, bales of pepper and many other spices, drugs and ointments, and diaphanous textiles which Tiberius (of all people) at one time forbade to the Roman public as indecent. The serious drain of specie to India at the height of Roman extravagance under Nero, of which Pliny

74 Opposite: a Chalukyan king, probably Pulakesin II (608–42), receiving Persian envoys; from a wall-painting at Ajanta.

75 India's transparent fabrics, shown in a second-century sculp-ture.

complained, is attested also by the scale of the hoarded currency – chiefly of the first five Roman emperors – which has been found in South India. Roman articles, which may or may not have been carried in Indian ships, have been excavated in Indo-China.

A factor of importance in this trade expansion was the general discovery, between AD 40 and 50, of what had for some time been a secret well guarded by its possessors: the way to exploit the seasonal monsoon winds for direct passage between the mouth of the Red Sea and Southern India (see map, p. 13). This shortened to two months the journey to or from Alexandria – and the West was never to be nearer India during the next eighteen centuries – and fed the fortunes of the Malabar port of Musiris (later Cranganore). Southern wealth, however, had been built up in the age of coastal traffic, supplemented by the rough but active network of Deccan land routes, with its southern terminus at the Pandyan capital of Madurai. The *Periplus* makes clear the preponderance in its day of the more northerly outlets on both western and eastern coasts. Southern products were thus among the Indian exports passing to the Persian Gulf route through Barygaza (Broach, two hundred miles north of Bombay at the mouth of the Narbada), which in the first century AD was still the port best known to the Western world. In the same way ivories and silks from Bengal were available for trade in the South Indian markets, where colonies of Roman, Greek and other foreign merchants had been established.

The Indian links with South-East Asia had also developed during the coasting era, following the northern shore of the Bay of Bengal before turning south to the Irrawaddy delta. The first Indianized state in Cambodia was called Fu-nan in the Chinese annals, which date it from the first century AD. Within another hundred years commercial settlements in the Malay Peninsula were flourishing as Hindu kingdoms, and a major share in the trade with this area was eventually acquired by the South Indian Cholas. This Tamil dynasty, which gave its name to the Coromandel coast, was to have its day as a land and sea power that would be felt as far as Java. But the chief of

76 Indian ocean-going ship arriving in Java, from a frieze of the Borobodur stupa, eighth century AD.

several starting-points for the early Indian colonists was the tract in which the Godavari and Krishna rivers issue in the Bay of Bengal; and its history is that of the Andhra kingdom of the northern Deccan and its successors.

THE ANDHRA SUPREMACY

In the break-up of the Mauryan Empire, as has been seen, Central India from coast to coast fell to a new power. These Andhra rulers – known also by their dynastic name as Satavahanas – came of a Telugu-speaking, non-Aryan (or perhaps mixed) stock. Their line lasted for more than four centuries, but after their first conquests there was a fluctuating period in which they lost their north-western provinces to the Scythian Shakas, and they did not fully recover them until the first century A D. After that they had still to deal with the Shaka prince Rudradaman, who recorded in A D 150, at Junagadh in Saurashtra, his reconstruction and enlargement of a dam and canal works dating from Mauryan rule. The 'barbarian' use of Sanskrit in this early inscription is notable. So is the pragmatic matrimonial alliance with the Scythian prince's family which enabled the brahmanized Andhra dynasty, despite its proclaimed support of caste purity, to establish itself once more from Saurashtra on the Arabian Sea to the region of the later Madras on the south-east coast.

The acceptance by some thirty successive Andhra rulers of the Brahmanical sanctions of kingship was, as elsewhere, no bar to the patronage of Buddhist foundations. At Sanchi, which lies just north of the geographical Vindhya division, the extension of Andhra power is attested by an inscription assigning to the reign of one of its kings the magnificent gateways of the railing round the Great Stupa. Here the Andhra realm at its height marched with that of the Kushans, forming a channel for the artistic energy that accompanied the liberation of the Buddha figure. Stylistic influences from both Gandhara and Mathura, transmitted across the Deccan to the eastern coast, have been found in the draped image that from there reached the distant Celebes, along the sea routes of Indian trade and settlement.

The first Andhra capital was at Amaravati, in the Krishna-Godavari delta-lands beyond the gently sloping Eastern Ghats. The evidence of its flourishing in the vast Amaravati stupa would have vanished if the dramatically carved reliefs had not been rescued from the lime-burners and divided between the British Museum in London and the Madras Museum. Not far from Amaravati, an early Andhra city was in the third century A D rebuilt as a Buddhist centre and renamed Nagarjunakonda, though its association with the outstanding Mahayanist scholar Nagarjuna (a convert from a Deccan brahman family) is uncertain. It lies now, after the removal of important finds, under the reservoir of a hydroelectric project; but excavation since 1926 had revealed, besides the platform of a large stupa, the remains of twenty-seven monasteries and of a stadium and theatre, the designs of which have suggested, along with coin finds, an influential connection with Rome by way of the sea route.

77 Part of a relief from Amaravati illustrating the Buddhist 'Annunciation': the Buddha's mother, Maya, has a dream foretelling the birth of her son.

78 This relief from the great cultural centre of Nagarjunakonda shows the Amaravati stupa and the worship of the Buddha.

On the western side of the Andhra domain a different geology – the workable basaltic lavas formerly known as the Deccan trap – invited the Indian speciality of excavated architecture, from the cell retreats of Ashokan times through the cave-cathedral at Karle (dedicated in AD 120) to the eighth-century Kailasha temple at Ellura and the rock-cut halls and monasteries (a few of them Jain) that multiplied over many centuries. Their inscribed records of benefactions support other indications of the decentralized Andhra system: a pattern based on village self-government and, in the towns, a vigorous guild structure, headed by merchants and deciding in professional assemblies the regulation of work and wages, fixed-interest investment in trade, and the collection and use of charitable funds.

Of about a thousand of these hewn chambers, at scattered and rugged sites but always near the passes of the north-western Deccan, the Ajanta group of more than thirty, around a horseshoe gorge, has the greatest renown. The survival in haunting remnants of their once glowing profusion of mural-painting provides historical detail in costume and furnishing, ceremonial and daily life; more especially of the refinement

79 Ajanta: part of the gorge from which more than thirty monastic cave-chambers of worship, assembly and residence were cut and decorated over a period of a thousand years, from the second century BC to the eighth century AD.

of royal and upper-class luxury in which the Buddha theme and the *Jataka* stories are often enveloped. The caves span some ten centuries, and the paintings reveal, in aesthetic terms, a remarkable continuity of achievement. The northern 'Golden Age' of the Guptas was evidently the accumulation of several centuries of advance to which the Deccan had notably contributed. While writers of known southern origin (such as Dandin) took part in the Sanskrit efflorescence ascribed to the imperial Guptas, the Satavahana rulers of the wide Andhra territories, who never called themselves emperors, encouraged the more popular Prakrit literature; but of this not much has survived except in Sanskrit translations.

REGIONAL CONFLICTS

The Satavahanas faded from the scene towards the end of the third century A D, and it was under their successors, the Vakatakas of Berar, that the closer links developed with the Gupta Empire. With the fragmentation of that empire under the strain of the Hun invasions, peninsular history also became for long periods a confusing record of dynastic strife. To the distant view these 'battles of the kites and crows' appear interminably wasteful and pointless, large armies being used to compel vassalage or secure revenues, or indeed for the sake of the exercise and to boast, as did one Chalukya ruler, that he had fought 108 battles in twelve years. Another, growing too old for the business, ceremonially drowned himself in a sacred river to the sound of appropriate music.

It was the Chalukyas who re-established in the Deccan a kingdom strong enough (under Pulakesin II, 608–42) to check Harsha's attempted southward conquest, and important enough to exchange ambassadors with the Persian court. Though supplied by their brahman publicists with a respectably Aryan pedigree, they almost certainly had more recent Central Asian origins in the Gurjaras, a people who had entered India with the Huns and contributed also to the mixed stock of the Rajputs. The backbone of the Chalukyan state was formed by the Western Ghats, running for some 350 miles between their northern and southern capitals, Nasik and Badami. When Hsuan-tsang's travels brought him to Nasik he described Pulakesin II as a kshatriya of 'large and profound ideas' and 'beneficent actions', obeyed by his contented subjects 'with perfect submission'. Badami in the south had the aspect of a rocky stronghold several times lost and retaken. Its constellation of now abandoned shrines includes some of the earliest stone structures (as distinct from excavations) of India's religious architecture, with features suggesting the first steps towards both the Northern and Southern styles.

In 642 the death of Pulakesin, in battle with his Pallava rivals of the east coast, produced a division of the Chalukyas into eastern and western branches, of which the latter was replaced a century later by the Rashtrakutas, one of their feudatory clans. The Rashtrakutas, who maintained themselves till 973 before succumbing to a Chalukya revival, were prominent during that time in an inter-regional struggle too well

80 Opposite: the southern stronghold of the Chalukyas at Badami, taken and retaken in wars with the Pallavas and Rashtrakutas during two centuries, is today a village surrounded by early temples, caves and a sacred lake.

81, 82 Above and opposite: two eighth-century masterpieces of Hindu art in the Deccan. The Kailasha temple at Ellura (above) was excavated downwards out of the living rock to a depth of 100 feet for the Rashtrakuta King Krishna I; the gigantic triple head of Shiva (opposite) in his creative, preservative and destructive aspects, broods in the Elephanta cave on an island in the inlet of Bombay.

balanced to allow any of the contestants to achieve a unitary power. In the North the pattern of conflict among the ruins of the Gupta Empire had produced since the death of Harsha an east-west confrontation of the Palas of Bengal with the mixed strain of early Rajput clans known as the Pratiharas. And in this fluctuating contest for the old capitals of power, with Kanauj the symbolic prize, the Rashtrakutas at one period made their own bid from the south. Under Govinda III (783–815) – when the shadow of a new contestant had already appeared with the Arab conquest of Sind – they defeated the Palas in Bengal and advanced to the slopes of the Himalayas; and though they had soon to withdraw, their raid had its political effect.

On their own ground the Rashtrakutas left their most extraordinary memorial in the great Kailasha temple among the Ellura caves, larger and much more complex than the Parthenon and excavated in its entirety, including some of the finest of Indian figure-sculpture, downwards in the living rock from the top of the hillside. This stupendous work of art was carried out by command of the Rashtrakuta ruler Krishna I (c. 756–73). His later successors turned from the worship of Vishnu to adopt the Jain teachings. But the last of the great cave-temples, on the island of Elephanta near Bombay, is by some assigned to the end of the Rashtrakuta era in the western Deccan. It was to survive the iconoclasm of the sixteenth-century Portuguese (it is said) because of the awe inspired in Trinitarian Christians by the gigantic three-faced Shiva head (*Trimurti*) that broods out of the darkness of this noble shrine.

Mystery and dispute obscure the origin of the Pallavas of the eastern coastal region, whose persistent rivalry had in the seventh century worn down the first Chalukyan kingdom of the Deccan plateau. It is reasonably clear that this first significantly Tamil dynasty contained alien as well as tribal strains, but the adoption of caste principles and an Aryan genealogy was carried in their case to the length of claiming the supreme deity Brahma as an ancestor. Towards the end of the ninth century, weakened by a reviving branch of the Chalukyas, the Pallavas gave way to the rising power of the empire-building Cholas. But before they did so they had transmitted the special cult of a god-king across the ocean to that kingdom of Fu-nan which in the seven centuries of its existence had been deeply indebted to Indian influence. Fu-nan fell to the Khmers at the same point as the Pallava decline, but bequeathed the divine

83 Detail from *The Descent of the Ganges*, a relief 30 feet high carved on the natural rock-wall of a reservoir at Mamallapuram.

kingship to Yasovarman I (889–910), whose first Angkor capital centred upon the Indian symbol of a 'mountain-temple', with the Shiva-lingam at the heart of its cult.

The first wave of overseas influence from the Pallava capital of Kanchi (Conjeevaram), however, had had the religious complexion of Hina-yana Buddhism. Jainism also was protected by the early Pallavas; but the advance of Brahmanism in a popular Tamil form, propagated by itinerant minstrel-saints, was recognized and promoted after Mahendra-varman I (600–630) was converted to the cult of Shiva. On the now deserted shore site of Mamallapuram, once a Pallava port, a group of temples hewn directly from the granite boulder outcrop stands beside the immense rock-face bas-relief called *The Descent of the Ganges*, and cul-minates on the ocean's edge in the prototype of a structured temple (*c.* 700). A similar Shiva temple was to begin the transformation of near-

84 The shore-temple at Mamalla-puram, the only structured build-ing in a complex of shrines and monuments cut from monoliths *in situ*, is the earliest model of a purely Dravidian temple-form.

by Kanchi from a place of Buddhist pilgrimage into the Brahmanical sacred city of 'a thousand temples and ten thousand shrines'; and Mamallapuram was echoed, six hundred miles to the north-west across the Deccan, in that Kailasha excavation of the Rashtrakutas. All these, in the words of Dr Benjamin Rowland, are 'creations of the Dravidian imagination in its finest hour of artistic expression'.

To the Dravidian religious imagination and the Dravidian intellect Hindu India owes, from this same period, the reinvigoration of the Vedic tradition that had become arid and diffuse in the expanded *Aryavarta* of the North. Shankara or Shankaracharya, who has been called 'the Brahman Aquinas', was born about 790 in the country of the Cheras on the south-western coast (now Kerala) in a cosmopolitan climate long hospitable to Christians, Jews and Arabs. In a life of thirty or forty years he developed, and propagated far and wide, a regenerated orthodoxy that combined a pruning and simplification of the ritual overgrowth of Brahmanism with a brilliant systemization of Upanishadic utterance (the *Vedanta*) as the substance of a philosophical

doctrine (*Advaita*, or monism) which could combat intellectual Buddhism by usurping some of its ground. He set up an order to continue his work, and his travels through the subcontinent to establish its posts as pilgrim centres at the four extreme points of the compass are a remarkable evidence of the mobility of the period. An early effect of Shankara's decisive influence was to strengthen the trend among ruling kshatriyas to accept the status value of the Shaivite (Shiva) cult, to the further detriment of Buddhist and Jain standing in the South.

In South-East Asia the flux of states and dynasties of Indian origin and Indianized development, from their remote beginnings in Champa and Fu-nan, had by the ninth century produced not only the Khmer power in Cambodia, its vivid culture profoundly inspired by Brah-manism, but also the Indonesian empire of the Shailendras – probably of Orissan ancestry – whose commercial domination went hand-in-hand with Mahayana Buddhism. The growth of Shailendra hegemony, from the settlements in the Malay Peninsula to those in Java and Bali, had now reached Sumatra, with a transfer of the capital from famed

85 Borobodur in Central Java, the supreme Buddhist monument of Greater India, is both stupa and cosmic mountain, constructed in five stepped terraces, profusely carved with reliefs. It dates from the eighth century, early in the Shailendra hegemony.

83

86 A Chola king: thirteenth-century bronze.

Borobodur to Shrivijaya (Palembang). The Buddhist monuments of Borobodur are of a grandeur hardly to be matched in India itself. But the tropical phenomenon of 'Greater India' has to be distinguished from the wider process of Buddhist diffusion with which it was at one time represented as merging. The Brahmanical elements which underlay and in some areas supplanted the Buddhist missionary impulse in this region, and the pervasive base of a transplanted Sanskrit, constitute a unique example of Hindu cultural expansion. As with other overseas empires, trade was a dominating factor. But state power and policies were from early stages involved at the source, and political organizations were the product. It is the Pallavas, who had a navy to protect their commerce, who are first seen to be fully committed to the political theme. As a 'mother-country', however, the Pallava kingdom was regional and beset by rivals, while the overseas states and empires became self-generating. Only a secure supremacy on the mainland could give full meaning to a Greater India; yet it followed also that, when the Cholas of Tanjore, who had been vassals of the Pallavas, achieved such a position, their empire came into collision with the main Indianized power in South-East Asia.

THE EMPIRE OF THE CHOLAS

The Cholas, in the awestruck words of a Tamil poet, 'watered their war-elephants in the Ganges'. The expedition that advanced so far to the north was a shortlived affair, but at its greatest extent in the eleventh century their empire did cover the peninsula, south of a diagonal from the region of the later Goa on the west coast to Orissa on the east. Once in possession of a continuous seaboard in the south, they attacked the commercial competition of the Arabs by occupying the Maldive and Laccadive Islands and the northern half of Ceylon. This took place under the great Chola ruler Rajaraja I (985–1014). His successor, Rajendra I (1014–44) moved to attack the long-standing problem of piracy in the Malacca Straits, and to secure the rich trade to the islands and to China by a grip on key-points in Malaya, Sumatra and Java.

Here the Cholas were challenging the sprawling Shailendra power, but their tactical purposes seem to have been partially achieved without disabling the Shailendra Empire, which indeed survived their own, only to be gradually undermined by the new force of Islamic expansion and to lose its long domination to the seagoing Portuguese at the end of the fifteenth century. The anciently Indianized kingdom of Champa (in modern times represented by South Vietnam) fell in the same epoch, overwhelmed by an early example of the north–south drive in that area. In eastern Java, however, a late Hindu state called Majapahit maintained itself for another century, leaving the Bali dance-culture as a legacy.

In their own domain the Cholas strengthened the foundations of a society that was to show powers of endurance. The village unit was allowed exceptional autonomy, conducting its affairs through elected committees and spending a proportion of the land-tax for its own purposes, while the state invested largely in irrigation works. The tax assessments were based on periodical surveys, establishing a pattern of customary rights which eventually inspired British administrators in the Madras Presidency to resist the extension to South India of the landlordism inherent in Lord Cornwallis's 'Permanent Settlement' for Bengal of 1793. This direct association of the state with the cultivator (it did not apply in the Deccan, where feudatories intervened) was accompanied under the Cholas by a continuation of the Pallava land-gifts to brahmans, whose advancing power had less happy consequences. Nowhere else did the caste system come to bear so hardly as in South India upon shudras, outcastes and landless labourers.

A contemporary protest against the exclusion of the lowest orders was voiced by the eleventh-century Tamil brahman Ramanuja, revered like Shankara as a Dravidian gift to the whole Hindu world. A Vaishnavite (follower of Vishnu), Ramanuja set against Shankara's eloquent monism a spiritual philosophy which distinguished between the universal absolute and the individual soul, thus sanctioning the concept of love between God and man. The devotional momentum (*bhakti*) for which he provided a theology did more than exalt the cult of Krishna as Vishnu's popular incarnation. It strengthened the power to resist the later appeal of Christian conversion, and it enriched Tamil literature as a vehicle for preserving the abundant celebration of its regional saints by wandering minstrels.

The Chola monarchs were declared Shaivites, and great builders. The great temple raised by Rajaraja I in his capital of Tanjore exemplifies the Dravidian development of an inner temple-city, populous in its own establishment and a fortress-shelter in emergency. It provided among other things for four hundred dancing-girls, exponents of the exacting art of *Bharata Natyam* and not yet degraded from ritualistic to promiscuous sexuality. Another art perfected at this time was that of the South Indian craftsman in *cire-perdue* metal sculpture, having as its chief glory the bronzes of the cosmic dance of Shiva (Nataraja, or Lord of the Dance).

Among the seceding Deccan chieftains who weakened the Chola position during the twelfth century, the most effective were the Hoysalas of the Mysore plateau, whose success encouraged a revival of the Pandyas of Madurai, in the ancient kingdom of India's southern tip. Supplanting the Cholas as the dominant Tamil power, the Pandyas also broke the Hoysalas, and advanced to a prosperity much admired by the Venetian Marco Polo on his visits in 1288 and 1293 from the Chinese court of Kublai Khan. But it was a brief glory, ended by a succession dispute which in 1311 woke the South to the existence of a new factor in history when it allowed a force sent by a Delhi sultan to sack Madurai before returning to the North. Dravidian resistance thereafter found another champion in the mighty Hindu kingdom of Vijayanagar, named after its mid-Deccan capital ('City of Victory') founded on the Tungabhadra river in 1336. From here the Vijayanagar power established itself over the whole southern peninsula, a bulwark against Islamic expansion that held until the sixteenth century.

87 A Chola queen: thirteenth-century bronze.

85

CHAPTER SIX

The Impact of Islam

ARABS AND GHAZNAVIDS

The Prophet Mohammad had died in AH 10 of the new era dated from his flight to Medina, or by our reckoning in AD 632. Only eighty years later an Arab empire stretched from the Pyrenees to the Indus valley. The Arab conquest of Sind in 712, however, did not of itself point towards an Islamic Indian supremacy. It was an isolated operation, distinct even in its point of entry, not by any of the northerly passes but by the Makran coastal route of Alexander's withdrawal, and then up the Indus to a hard-fought victory at Brahmanabad.

For many centuries Arab seamen and merchants had been familiar to the Indians of the western coasts, and numbers of them had settled in Malabar. Armed intrusion was another matter, and the Chalukyan rulers of Gujarat took steps to defend their territories against any southward move from Sind. They also welcomed Zoroastrians escaping from forcible conversion under the Arab subjugation of Persia, and these refugees became the founders of the Parsi community. In the northern Punjab the limits of Arab rule were set by a currently powerful Hindu kingdom of Kashmir. On the east, where Kashmiri military adventure penetrated spasmodically as far as Bengal, the putative defenders of India were those splendid mongrels afterwards renowned as Rajputs, and at this time as Gurjara-Pratiharas. Though they repelled a few Arab probings in the desert area, the gaze of these Pratihara Rajputs was mainly eastward, their preoccupation a wasteful conflict for the faded dream of empire in the Gangetic plain.

Within their substantial but circumscribed domain, the Arab rulers of Sind showed no signs of the proselytizing zeal with which the Umayyad Caliph of Damascus had dispatched them, but declared and practised religious toleration, retaining brahman and other Indian officials in their administration. When the aggressive generation of the Umayyads gave way to the brilliant Abbasid period in Baghdad, that cultural clearing-house welcomed the transmission through Sind of the Indian contribution to learning. It was in the last quarter of the eighth century that the earlier Indian work in astronomy and mathematics, and the all-important Indian numerical system, reached Baghdad, to be followed a little later by the decimal system of place-value. Tainted by their infidel source, the new numbers were not accepted in Christendom until three or four centuries later.

By 871 Sind had become politically detached from the Caliphate. There was no Indian inspiration for a crusading enterprise such as the

88 Opposite: Kutb Minar, Delhi, the 240-foot-high tower of victory begun by Kutb-ud-din Aibak, founder of the Slave Dynasty, early in the twelfth century and completed by Firoz Shah Tughluq in the fourteenth.

89 Persian wheel irrigation, an Islamic introduction into India, as were paper, gunpowder and the true arch.

Christian West undertook in the eleventh century, for there was no Holy Land to rescue, the regions of the earliest Aryan colonization having ceased to be so regarded by the orthodox after a thousand years of alien intrusions – and more emphatically since the Hun pollution. The idea of the barbarian *mlechcha* as impure in the same degree as the non-Aryan aboriginal was renewed by the Brahmanical revival; but xenophobia remained paradoxically associated with the facility for assimilating foreigners. This gave the unique institution of caste, as a relationship that cut across all others, its remarkable preservative power. In the military sphere the Rajputs were to be formed into Wardens of the Marches by caste alone, welded out of different non-Aryan materials into a martial society of interrelated families, and rewarded with kshatriya status and certificates of descent from the sun or moon. In their Pratihara stage the long three-cornered contest with the Rashtrakutas of the Deccan and the Palas of Bengal had left them, by the early tenth century, exhausted and unstable masters of the North.

To hungry eyes beyond the north-western passes, however, there seemed to be plenty left for the picking:

The whole country of India is full of gold and jewels, and of the plants which grow there are those fit for making apparel, and aromatic plants and the sugar-cane, and the whole aspect of the country is pleasant and delightful. Now, since the inhabitants are chiefly infidels and idolators, by the order of God and his Prophet it is right for us to conquer them.

Such, said his chroniclers, was the decision reached by Sultan Mah‑
mud of Ghazni, who over the first quarter of the eleventh century
inflicted on Northern India an estimated total of seventeen invasions.
The Ghaznavids were Turki‑speaking Central Asian converts to
Islam who had advanced from slaves and mercenaries of the Caliphate
to be masters of an expanding Afghan principality which under
Mahmud became an empire stretching from the Caspian to the Pun‑
jab. His main interests lay to the west and north across the valuable
trade lines. What concerned India was the speed with which he
could plunge into its plains for the spoils with which he returned
to extend and protect his Bactrian and Persian frontiers. His mixed
forces were ferocious in war and in plunder, and he knew how to
use the light cavalry of the steppelands against the often larger armies
of his opponents and the ponderous phalanx of elephants that was
still the pride of India's battlefields. Massacre and destruction marked
his path, slaves of both sexes were carried off by the hundred thousand,
temples and treasuries were looted. He penetrated to the heart of
Hindustan, to Kanauj on the Ganges, to Mathura (whose splendours
he much admired before erasing them), and finally through the
desert to Saurashtra and the fabulously rich temple of Somnath
on the coast, where fifty thousand Hindus were put to the sword and
the great shrine was despoiled and defiled. This was in 1023, and by
1030 Mahmud was dead. A part of the Punjab and Lahore remained
in Ghaznavid possession; but during the next 150 years, until a new

90 The marble tomb of Mahmud
'the Idol‑Breaker', in his Afghan
capital of Ghazni, obeys Koranic
orthodoxy in avoiding all decora‑
tion save calligraphy and abstract
pattern.

conqueror, Muhammad Ghuri (of Ghor), established himself in Ghazni, India was spared the fury of invasion.

Mahmud's lasting reputation as 'the Idol-Breaker' would hardly have been earned if so much wealth in gold and jewels had not been concentrated in the temples. A part of these bloodily-acquired spoils went to the embellishment of Ghazni with a university and libraries and the upkeep of a cultured court, of which the foremost Persian poet Firdausi was one of the lights. Another was the historian, mathematician and astronomer Al Biruni, learned in Persian, Arabic, Greek and Sanskrit, who compiled an account of North Indian ways and conditions in his time.

THE FEUDAL SCENE IN THE NORTH

Allied with the rising power of the brahmans, the Rajput clan system submerged earlier relationships in a feudalistic pattern of land-grants to vassals, to whose military obligations there were added those of remitting the 'king's share' of the revenue and of preserving law and order. The land-taxes, which struck Al Biruni as light, were not so in practice. The brahmans, who had been the first recipients of land-gifts, were exempt from taxation, which thus fell the more heavily upon the estates of kshatriya feudatories. As hereditary holding overtook the theory of devising only the life-income, and not the land itself, the pyramid of intermediaries supported by the cultivators tended to solidify. Temple dues and unpaid labour were additional burdens, and the curse of the rural moneylender (with shudras liable for thrice the interest charged to brahmans) was beginning to be felt. Subsistence farming – a token of the village's retreat under stress – played its part in the shrinkage of internal trade. The decline of Buddhist institutions and the migration of Jain influence towards the western coast (neither sect receives more than a mention from Al Biruni) had their economic reflection in urban stagnation. The vaishya middle-class lost status, and a proliferation of sub-castes weakened the network of trade guilds. The products of craftsmen maintained their traditional quality, but had to bear something like a value-added tax.

Rajput chivalry exalted principles of honour and equity, and could dispense with oppressive legislation. Al Biruni, indeed, thought that the laws were too mild, since 'the manners and customs of the Hindus resemble those of the Christians' in recognizing unrealistic propositions of human virtue. The customs which honoured and to some degree protected women – and even educated some of them – also imposed upon the households of chieftains the rite of the *sati* (see p. 68 and ill. 73), with its lower-class alternative of degraded widowhood. Child-marriage and female infanticide were likewise encouraged by a militaristic social pattern.

As a stranger and a Muslim, Al Biruni took note of an anthropomorphic religion, demonstrated in pilgrimages to sacred rivers (Banaras being now the chief site) and spawning a multiplicity of gods presided over by a trinity which he likened to that of the Christians. He observed, however, that those of higher education believed in a single, transcendental and yet all-pervading deity. In the state of brahman scholarship he was struck by the dilution of genuine learning with wild superstitions, the mixture being frozen by an insular disdain and ignorance of the science and ideas of other countries. 'Their ancestors were not so narrow-minded as the present generation.'

It is a telling charge, though record exists of shining exceptions by rulers (for instance Raja Bhoja of Malwa, 1018–60, and others of his line) whose courts were distinguished centres of learning and the arts. Time and iconoclasm have decimated the architectural evidence in Northern India, but in what remains Bundelkhand can show – thanks to the astuteness of its ruler when destruction threatened – the magnificent group of temples at Khajurao (950–1050). In the Mahanadi delta in Orissa, an area hallowed from prehistoric times, a continuity of temple-building from the eighth to the thirteenth centuries is displayed in a trio of renowned centres: Bhuvaneshwar, with some five hundred lakeside shrines, large and small, out of a legendary total of seven thousand; Puri, still in use and exclusive, less remarkable after several reconstructions, and dedicated to Vishnu-Jaganath (the 'juggernaut' of the car festival); and Konarak, with its breathtaking chariot-temple to the sun-god Surya, massively raised – though never completed – under King Narasimha of the Ganga dynasty. Achievements such as these cannot have been isolated; and they astonish – so far from bespeaking decadence – by the creative imagination which could transcend the elaborate canonical traditions that have always governed Hindu art. It may be added that the theme of sexuality in the *mithuna* figures, however it may be interpreted, had a sculptural ancestry of at least a thousand years.

91 Decorated reverse of a copper plate recording a land-grant in Bengal, 1196. A cultivator appeals to the god Vishnu.

NORTHERN MEDIEVAL TEMPLES

92, 93 Opposite, above: Khajurao presents a brilliant style of its own, both in architecture and in sculpture, typified by the detail of a *mithuna* or amatory couple. The Kandariya Mahadeo temple (left) is one of the finest in the group built between 950 and 1050.

94, 95 Opposite, below: *mithuna* couples appear also in the decoration of the culminating Orissan temple form, the great Lingaraja temple of the Bhuvaneshwar group (AD 1000), with its 140-foot-high *shikara* tower.

96, 97 Above, left and right: *mithuna* heads on the Jagannath temple at Puri, and the temple itself, which is still in use.

98 Right: one of the carved chariot-wheels of the unique temple of the sun-god Surya at Konarak, final achievement of the Orissan builders in the mid-thirteenth century.

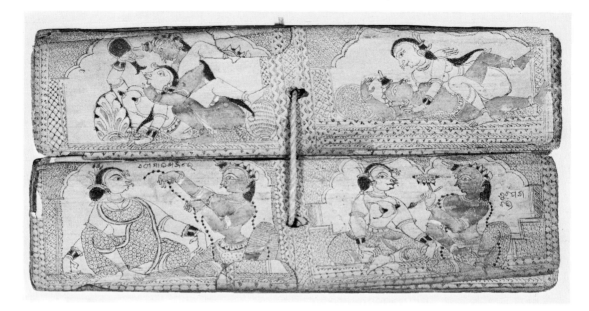

99 Krishna and Radha as lovers,
on a palm-leaf manuscript of the
Gita Govinda made about 1600.

The Shiva cult had by now taken over from the Buddhist laity in Bengal those magical practices of Tantrism, of obscure antiquity, which under the Pala protectors of Buddhism had been cross-fertilized with Tibet. The Senas who succeeded the Palas were a Hindu dynasty, and although the power rites of the Tantric sect were occult and secret, they preserved within the Hindu fold a valid spirit of revolt in their disregard of caste, class and sex restrictions. On the Vaishna-vite side the wide open, mystically sensuous and powerfully pervasive role of Krishna in Indian religion, and thus in Indian painting (paper was a Muslim introduction) and sculpture, dance, song and literature, can also be dated from this period. Its classic presentation in the San-skrit *Gita Govinda* of Jayadeva, emanating from Bengal but already owing something to the *bhakti* movement in Hinduism spreading from the South (see p. 102), appeared at the end of the twelfth century, at the very point of Northern India's first effective subjection to Islamic conquest.

The real weaknesses that invited alien occupation, as distinct from the Sind side-issue and from plundering raids, were political and military. Internal rivalries were abetted, rather than dissolved, by the quixotic pageantries of an aristocratic Rajput war-game. If the lessons of successive defeats by Mahmud of Ghazni had ever been learned, they had been forgotten by 1192, when the next scourge appeared. In that year Muhammad Ghuri, having overrun the former Ghaznavid dependencies in the Punjab and acquired the suzerainty over what was left of Arab Sind, brought Rajput chivalry to a fresh challenge at Taraori, on the historic plain of Panipat. A combination of forces had, it is true, come together for once under Prithviraj III, of the now leading Rajput clan of the Chauhans of Ajmer. It had even repulsed Muhammad and his Afghans, in the year before Taraori, on much the same battlefield. But the defensive unity was not complete, and there had been further defections before the Ghuri warrior came back for vengeance with an increased army of mixed adventurers. Prithviraj, captured and executed after thousands of his followers had perished, passed from decisive defeat into romantic immortality. So, on the funeral pyre with her attendants, did the Queen whom as a princess he had carried off across his saddle-bow, in Lochinvar fashion, from the court of an unforgiving Rajput rival.

THE TURCO-AFGHAN PARAMOUNTCY

The Afghan victory opened the way to Prithviraj's cities of Ajmer, where the temples were obliterated and a great mosque raised, and Delhi, now for the first time to become an important capital: though not of a Ghuri empire from the Oxus to the Bay of Bengal such as Muhammad may have envisaged, for he had soon to return beyond the Hindu Kush to confront his enemies in Western Asia. The reduction of the states of the Gangetic plain down to Banaras – which fell without a fight, for its shrines and treasures to suffer the usual fate – was undertaken by his Turki slave and chief general, Kutb-ud-din Aibak. Beyond Banaras another Muslim general accomplished independently and without difficulty the conquest of Bihar and Bengal, dealing to India's remaining Buddhist centres the last savage blow, with the slaughter or dispersal of the monks. When Muhammad was assassinated in 1206, his gains in Northern India passed to the faithful Kutb-ud-din, whereby the first sultans or kings of Delhi became known to history as the Slave Dynasty.

100 Chinghiz Khan receiving homage, seen in a Persian miniature. His descent into India was fortunately brief.

For the next three centuries the Slave Dynasty and its successors provided, with Delhi as the source of a fluctuating authority, the story of

> How Sultan after Sultan with his pomp
> Abode his destined hour, and went his way.

The witness to their ambitions survives in the tombs and monuments, the isolated mosques and abandoned citadels, scattered over the strategic plain between the Jumna river and the last spur of the Aravalli hills, near to the site on which Moghul Delhi was afterwards to set its imperial stamp, and today invaded by the expansion of the late British New Delhi into the capital of a federal Indian Republic. As the first of the sultans the slave-general Aibak had only four years before he died in 1210, but he left his mark in two of the finest constructions of these early Delhis: the Kwat-ul-Islam mosque in its first form, and the lower storey of the Kutb Minar, the unique victory-tower eventually completed by his successors to its planned height of 240 feet.

Aibak also left to the second sultan, Iltutmish (1211–36), who was his son-in-law, the task of consolidating the dynasty's precarious hold on Northern India, in a series of campaigns against rebellion in the Punjab, Rajput recalcitrants in Gwalior and Malwa, tribesmen in the north-west, and his own general's bid for independent power in Bengal. It was in the reign of Iltutmish also that Chinghiz (Genghiz) Khan, having united the Mongol Tartars into an instrument of world conquest, swept down to the Indus in pursuit of one of his fleeing foes. Fortunately he had business elsewhere, and vanished again, but there was a dangerous period of anarchy after the death of Iltutmish until another slave-general, Balban, secured the Sultanate (1266–87) and restored control of Northern India by the merciless severity of his punitive expeditions and the iron efficiency of an administration supported by a far-reaching system of state spies.

Although the Mongol Hulagu, after his capture and destruction of Baghdad, promised that there would be no more raids into India, other pressures led to their renewal. With the general adoption of Islam by the Mongols at the end of the thirteenth century, numbers of them were allowed to settle in the upper reaches of the Jumna and the Ganges. At this date the Slave Dynasty had been succeeded in the Delhi Sultanate by the Afghan Khiljis, the strongest of whom was Ala-ud-din (1296–1316). It was Ala-ud-din who, as mentioned in the previous chapter, sent a force into the Deccan and as far south as Madurai. He is also remembered for the rigour of his rule and his campaigns against the Rajputs, in which the legendary stronghold of Chitor suffered its first capture. But the converted Mongols, unreliable as settlers, mutinous as soldiers, and at one point (1299) expanding

101 Hindu columns from devastated temples, incorporated in the halls of the Kwat-ul-Islam mosque at Delhi, begun in 1193.

raiding and immigration into attempted conquest at the gates of Delhi, were a greater and more hated threat, to be dealt with by extermination. Their leader was blinded, their children massacred, their wives given to the sweepers of Delhi and their surviving fighting men publicly trampled to death by elephants. Their kind had been the scourge of Asia, and more particularly of their Turki relatives, and they were so served. The Turki general most active in defeating the Mongol menace became, as Ghiyas-ud-din Tughluq I (1320–25), the first of the Tughluq line that followed the Khiljis in the Sultanate.

The significance of the Mongols for Indian history lies outside India. By demolishing the world from which Turks and Afghans had descended into India as soldiers of fortune, they compelled them to find their power-centre in the new land, and to organize their conquests accordingly. In the same process the influx of fresh blood from the parent stocks was reduced to a trickle, or replaced by a Mongol stream that had to be forcefully staunched. Assimilation and acclimatization in some degree thus became imperative, but the trend was gradual. Despite the extended military exploits of Ala-ud-din Khilji, the idea of a permanent empire ruled from Delhi first took hold in the House of Tughluq. The realm of Muhammad bin Tughluq (1325–51) was comparable at its furthest reach with the empire of Ashoka in the dim

102 Walls of the fort at Tughluqabad, the third city of Delhi, founded by Ghiyas-ud-din Tughluq but soon abandoned.

past or that of the Moghul Aurangzeb that was yet to come: and in the course of its construction it became apparent that it could *not* be ruled from Delhi.

Muhammad bin Tughluq, described by the Moorish traveller Ibn Batuta as 'a man who above all others is fond of making presents and shedding blood', had acceded by one of the more singular devices of an age rich in assassinations. To welcome his father, Ghiyas-ud-din, returning from a victorious campaign, he had erected a splendid pavilion, secretly and successfully designed by his engineer to collapse fatally upon the Sultan at the first tread of his elephant. Bizarre stories are also related of Muhammad's transference, not only of his court and government but of the entire population of Delhi to Deogiri, renamed Daulatabad, seven hundred miles to the south and thus convenient for his Deccan conquests. But if the Deccan could not be governed from Delhi, neither could Hindustan from Daulatabad, and the whole operation had eventually to be reversed. The re-established and re-populated capital on the Delhi plain was embellished by Muhammad's successor, Firoz Shah Tughluq (1351–88), with, among other things, one of the edict-pillars of Ashoka. Laboriously transported from a distant site, its inscription the more numinous for being then indecipher-able, the column bestowed upon Delhi the prestige of a misty antiquity of power. In his long and on the whole admirable reign Firoz Shah was credited with the erection of 200 towns, 40 mosques, 30 colleges, 30 reservoirs, 50 dams, 100 hospitals, 100 public baths and 150 bridges. He certainly founded the city of Jaunpur, on the Gumti, which became for a time a great centre of Islamic culture and the hotly con-tested capital of a rival kingdom. But to claim the paramountcy, even in the last phases of the Sultanate's decline, it was always necessary to hold Delhi.

The centrifugal tendencies which Firoz Shah, a ruler of principled mildness, forbore to meet with force, had shown under the excessive ambitions of the previous reign that force could not control them. Before Muhammad died Bengal had become an independent Muslim kingdom, and the southern provinces and their revenues had been lost in a chain of rebellions, culminating in the establishment of the Bah-mani state of the western Deccan by one of the Sultan's dissident officers, and the foundation of the Hindu power of Vijayanagar to the south of it. Khandesh, occupying the north–south divide formed by the Narbada and Tapti rivers, broke away from Firoz Shah's Sultanate, Malwa and Gujarat from the brief degeneracy of his successors. The Punjab governor was under no restraint, and Rajput chieftains were again stirring, when in 1398 Timur the Barlas Turk, the lame world-shaker known to the West as Tamerlaine, swept down through the lower Punjab, defeated a sizeable force that came out from Delhi to con-front him, and extracted a vast ransom for the city – which even so suf-fered a three-day sacking from his allegedly uncontrollable troops. 'All the artisans and clever mechanics who were masters of their respective trades' were by his own account spared to be sent as slaves to his capital, Samarkand.

103 The tomb of a great builder, Firoz Shah Tughluq (d. 1388), at his Delhi capital. It was restored early in the sixteenth century by order of Sikandar Lodi.

104 Timur was buried in this imperial mausoleum in Samarkand, his Central Asian capital, which was embellished by Indian craftsmen sent there as slaves after the sack of Delhi in 1398.

 بابر اکبر   جهانگیر همایون

105 Timur is commemorated in this Moghul miniature with four of his descendants in the imperial dynasty of India: at his right hand are seated Akbar and Babur, at his left Humayun and Jahangir.

Plunder and chastisement were enough for Timur's appetite. As a Muslim he was persuaded that the Hindu infidels were lawful prey, and a hundred thousand of them had been slaughtered after capture on the way to Delhi. Nor could the ruling class and their Muslim converts expect, as Sunnis, special favours from Timur, who was (as the Sind Arabs had been) a Shia. This persistent schism had its origins in the disputed succession to the Caliphate on a hereditary (Shia) as against an elective (Sunni) basis. In Delhi the Ulema (established theologians) and the Sayyids (who claimed an original descent from the Prophet) were untouched, but other Muslim prisoners were enslaved. There-after Timur soon lost interest in India and departed by a northerly route, spreading massacre and devastation through the Himalayan foothills. There was no conquest, but the visitation had a later political importance in enabling Babur, the first of the Moghuls, to claim the kingdom of Delhi by descent from Timur.

The last Tughluq, who had fled from the rout before Delhi, was able to return to the empty shell of power. After his death in 1414, an undistinguished line of Sayyids, beginning as Timur's deputies, called themselves sultans of Delhi for another thirty-seven years. The three Lodi kings who succeeded them (1451–1526) were Afghan soldier-administrators who after a time moved their capital to Agra, though they left their tombs among the dynastic relics of Delhi. Their writ ran nominally from the upper Punjab down to Bihar, but they were in the

hands of their factious nobles, whose dissensions let in Babur, the man of destiny, in 1526.

The regimes of the Delhi sultans in their rise and fall, with their off-spring of Muslim vassals, had had an impact necessarily different from anything produced by earlier invasions. Their temporal allegiance to the Caliphate, even before it was submerged by the Mongol deluge, was purely formal. They had to evolve their own polity in a land and among a people very different from those they had left, but the dynamic ideology which they brought with them precluded the kind of assimilation at which the Indian caste system had in the past proved adept. The sultans might, indeed must, employ brahman officials and tax-collectors, but they had their own theologians and their own jurists to sustain what was in practice a military despotism. Artillery was a Turkish innovation.

Rebellion was punished with new and revolting cruelties, especially by the Khilji Ala-ud-din and the Tughluq Muhammad – Firoz Shah abolished them for his time – but the power-game was largely played among the newcomers and there is little evidence of forced conversion, despite intermittent thunders against the infidels. The extent of volun-tary conversion is difficult to estimate, though it offered among practical advantages exemption from Islam's customary poll-tax upon un-believers. On the other hand the prospective yields of this tax dis-couraged most rulers (said their Muslim critics) from proselytizing. A move by Firoz Shah to end the tax-free privileges of the brahmans was

106 The Lodi kings were buried at Delhi in their native Pathan style, Sikandar Lodi under this double dome, an early example of the construction used afterwards by the Moghul builders.

101

met by passive resistance, and had to be commuted to a single small payment. There were periodical experiments in raising revenue, but no basic changes in the system or in that of land-grants and tenure. The administrative offices had new Persian or Arabic names, and Muslims at the top, but operated in much the old way.

With the dwindling of outside replenishment of the ruling class, its character was diluted by intermarriage with Indian women. Royal and noble harems of an extravagant size influenced the spread of the *pardah* system of feminine seclusion, and several sultans raised large bodies of male slaves, often employed as a private corps for political purposes. It was the Delhi sultans, also, who introduced workshops for the luxury crafts as a royal monopoly. The change from an armed camp to a court of cultural pretensions was affected by the influx of scholarly refugees from the hordes of Hulagu. The standards of civilization were Persian, and so was the official language which was to hold its place in Northern India, and with some extensions to the south, until the nineteenth century. This invasion of the status of Sanskrit promoted the development of the regional Indian languages. It was the Muslim rulers of Bengal who ordered the translation from Sanskrit to Bengali of the *Ramayana* and the *Mahabharata*; and the so-called 'camp language' of Urdu, as a working alternative, came of a marriage of Persian with Hindi, using in the written form not the Indian *devanagari* characters but the very different Arabic script.

The most esteemed of the Indo-Persian court poets, Ala-ud-din's librarian Amir Khusru, was a follower of one of the Indian orders of Sufism. This Persian mystical cult, though dissociated from Islamic orthodoxy, was not at this time persecuted as a heresy, and it reached India at just the point where it could find some common ground with the *bhakti* devotional movement (see p. 94). In Bengal and Bihar Jayadeva's poetical celebration of the Radha-Krishna theme was followed between the fourteenth and sixteenth centuries by Vidyapati, Chaitanya and Chandidas; Agra produced the blind poet Surdas, Rajasthan the wandering Princess Mirabai; in Maharashtra there were Muslim converts to Hinduism among the *bhakti* devotees. Of the twelve disciples of Ramananda, who brought Ramanuja's teaching from the South to Banaras and spread it in the Hindi vernacular, one was a barber, one a shoemaker, and one, Kabir (c. 1440–1518), a weaver brought up as a Muslim.

In Kabir's visionary verses Sufi and *bhakti* elements combine to insist that God is 'neither in temple nor in mosque . . . all the men and women in the world are His living forms'. His songs, handed down in their musical form, received their first translation into English in 1915 from the great Bengali poet Rabindranath Tagore. The egalitarian rejection of caste in Kabir's religious message, and his dissent from the priestly authority and ritualism of divisive creeds, are echoed in the similar teachings of Guru Nanak (1469–1539, a near contemporary of the German Luther). And these were to lead, under a subsequent pressure of Muslim persecution, to the forging of a new lever of Indian history: the Sikhs.

107 A Sufi hermit among the forest creatures. The Indian religious climate was congenial to this mystical sect, brought from Persia with the Muslim invasions of North India. To this day the tombs of Sufi saints are visited by Hindus and Muslims alike.

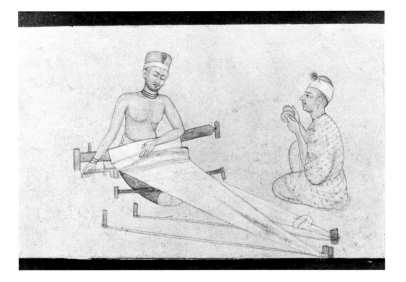

108 Kabir, the low-caste weaver inspired with a social as well as a religious message, working at his loom while a disciple sings.

CHAPTER SEVEN

Moghuls and Europeans

CHRISTIANS AND SPICES

The Portuguese arrived before the Moghuls. When Vasco da Gama, having rounded the Cape of Good Hope, crossed with his four ships (and an Indian pilot) to his Calicut landfall in 1498, Southern India acknowledged the Hindu supremacy of Vijayanagar. Northern India was divided between the rich Sultanate of Gujarat with its western outlets to the sea, a new Rajput confederacy led by Mewar, the Delhi Kingdom as remade by Ibrahim Lodi after the hammer-blows of Timur, and an independent Sultanate of Bengal. Between North and South the Muslim Bahmani power in the Deccan had split into three states, which presently became five: Bijapur and Ahmadnagar on the west, Golconda on the east, Bidar and Berar in the centre.

The southward pressure against Vijayanagar had produced warfare of a mutual and fanatical ferocity; but the Hindu empire was now touching its zenith, and its rulers were prepared to play off one hated sultanate against another by temporary alliances. Its capital 'City of Victory' fronted the Islamic enemy in the extreme north, but the wealth with which it dazzled the Italian traveller and physician Nicolo Conti flowed in from the peninsular coasts, from the territories of Hindu subsidiaries: such as the Zamorin of Calicut, 'King of the Mountains and the Sea', and first host to the ships of a Portuguese monarch ambitiously styled, with the backing of an exclusive Papal Bull, 'Lord of the Navigation, Conquest and Commerce of Ethiopia, Arabia, Persia and India'.

More simply, da Gama reported his objectives, in reply to the Zamorin, as 'Christians and spices'. The expected Christian establishment was a confusion with the Ethiopian legend of Prester John. The spices were, in the first place, the pepper and cardamom and other products of the Zamorin's small but important strip of the Malabar coast. Beyond that the prize was the monopoly of the trade with the spice-islands of the further East, of which Calicut had for centuries been a thriving centre. Control of the traffic which enriched not only the Zamorin and his overlord, but the merchants of Arabia, Egypt and the Persian Gulf, and finally of Venice, was seen as Portugal's economic reward for maritime progress and Christian zeal.

The Christians whom da Gama did find in Malabar – the so-called Syrian community – had been peacefully settled there for more than a thousand years. So had the Arabs, whose presence surprised and dismayed him. Unconnected with the Muslim sultanates to the north,

109 Opposite: Akbar, greatest of the Moghul emperors, consulting with divines whose religious rivalries he sought to harmonize in a syncretic 'Divine Faith'.

110 Vasco da Gama, whose first voyage round Africa to southern India opened in 1498 the era of European expansion in the East.

they were favoured by the Hindu Zamorin, whose dependence upon Arab commercial activity made him the only Indian ruler to react to the first signs of Portuguese aggressiveness. He also had links with the Sultan of Egypt, whose well-gunned vessels came to the aid of the Zamorin's outmatched coastal navy and put the Portuguese enterprise in some danger. The expeditions that followed Vasco da Gama failed to take Calicut, but established their first small strongpoint at near-by Cochin.

In 1509 Affonso Albuquerque began his masterly six years in command of the Portuguese interests in the East. Goa with its well-placed harbour was wrested from Bijapur, with Hindu assistance, in

GOA·

⚓ MORMV

CABO

ACO

111 'Golden Goa', shown in a map of 1646. The missionary aggressiveness of the Portuguese, which made enemies in India, was not shared by the traders of Holland, England, Denmark and France who succeeded them.

1510. The Sultan of Gujarat ceded another useful base, Diu, in dislike of the Arabs and fear of a Turco-Egyptian involvement. The Egyptian difficulty in replacing lost vessels (built with timber carried overland to the Red Sea) contrasted with the remarkable capacity of the Portuguese for regular reinforcement over the vast distance of their sea route. After the hard-fought capture of Malacca in 1511, Albuquerque completed his grand design with a strategic base at Ormuz, at the entrance to the Persian Gulf, and the seizure of Socotra Island (an attempt on Aden having failed) to supervise the Red Sea commerce. The spice trade was controlled at its main source in the East Indies, and the traffic of the Arabian Sea came under a Portuguese licensing system.

Indian policies were piecemeal and land-bound, and the Portuguese arrangement worked. Their control of the sea carriage of Mecca pilgrims was naturally resented, but they did not at first appear as a proselytizing force. Nor did they show territorial ambitions beyond their coastal bases – Albuquerque's aim of a permanent presence being satisfied by encouraging mixed marriages, the beginning of the hybrid community of Roman Catholic Goans. During the reign of Vijaya-nagar's greatest ruler, Krishnadeva Raya (1509–30), who cultivated good relations with Goa as a trade outlet and source of military supplies, the Portuguese did not persecute Hindus.

The change began in the 1540s, on orders from Lisbon. It was not the saintly missionary efforts of Francis Xavier and his followers that bred antagonism, but the savage treatment inflicted on non-conforming Indian Christians, as well as on Hindus within the Portuguese reach. In 1560 the Inquisition was established in Goa. The Portuguese decline, which was to set in after a century of prideful wealth and power, had primary causes in Europe, but the character that they showed in the East played its part.

THE FIRST FOUR MOGHULS

Babur had a formidable ancestry. Descended from Timur through his father and from Chinghiz Khan through his mother, he had struggled from boyhood to recover his Central Asian patrimony from the Uzbegs. Failing to hold Samarkand, he made Kabul a springboard for a descent, in the winter of 1525–6, into the North Indian lands which Timur had briefly conquered and which he regarded as his by right. The Lodi subordinate who had collaborated in the design left him unsupported to face, on the field of Panipat, the greatly superior forces of Ibrahim Lodi, who was killed in the famous battle that went Babur's way by brilliant generalship as much as by the use of artillery. Having proclaimed himself sultan at Delhi and Agra, Babur had to use his genius for personal leadership to dissuade his chiefs from return-ing, as summer approached, to the cooler hills of home. He had still to fight a Rajput confederacy led by the Mewar Rana Sangram Singh – or by what was left of him after eighty wounds, the loss of an eye and an arm, and a shattered leg, all sustained in victorious encounters with the Afghans. At Kanua the Rajput hopes of a Hindu restoration were once more left in ruins, and three years later Babur died in the Persian water-garden that he had laid out in Agra.

He was only forty-seven, and there is a favourite tale that he had asked God to take his life in exchange for that of his son Humayun, who there-upon recovered from a serious illness. The story fits Babur's character, frank and open-hearted, and combining the zest of living with a readi-ness to share the worst hardships and dangers of his men. His victories might be marked by towers of skulls, but he had none of Timur's savagery. His love of music, good company, and bibulous picnics, his fresh delight in natural beauty, are woven into the narrative excitement of his justly famed *Memoirs*. Nostalgia for the land of his birth made his remarks on India's people and products curiously denigrating, but his

درختهای انار هم هست کردا کرد حوض تمام سبزگزار

112 Babur laying out a water-garden – a favourite pursuit – in Kabul. From a Persian manu-script of his celebrated *Memoirs*, made for his grandson Akbar.

gifts could in a normal span have been well used in consolidating the realm that he had won, the fate of which under Humayun (1530–56) was in constant doubt. The most enigmatic of the Moghuls, Humayun alternated energy with phases of fatal irresolution (perhaps connected with the opium habit), treated his ambitious brothers with unwise clemency, and in the result spent most of his nominal reign as an exile under the protection of the Safavid Shah of Persia, his throne being meanwhile usurped by Sher Shah, an Afghan from Bengal. Happily Sher Shah displayed outstanding gifts as a soldier-statesman, and in the five years before he died justice and security were established, communi-cations improved, the currency stabilized and the revenue reassessed. His two Afghan successors proving worthless, Sher Shah's construc-tive achievement reverted to the Moghuls when in 1555 Humayun recovered Delhi, only to die six months later after falling downstairs from his library within the Delhi citadel (now called the Purana Qila) which Sher Shah had built. His widow raised for him the magnificent tomb, white marble and red sandstone, that confidently announced the glory of Timur's dynasty. But Humayun's chief memorial was to have fathered Akbar.

HUMAYUN (1508–1556)

113 Humayun on the throne which in 1540, after ten years, he had to abandon as a fugitive; he regained it fifteen years later, but with less than six months to live.

114 The Emperor forgiving his brother Kamran, flagrantly guilty of treachery. Humayun was finally forced by his nobles to blind him.

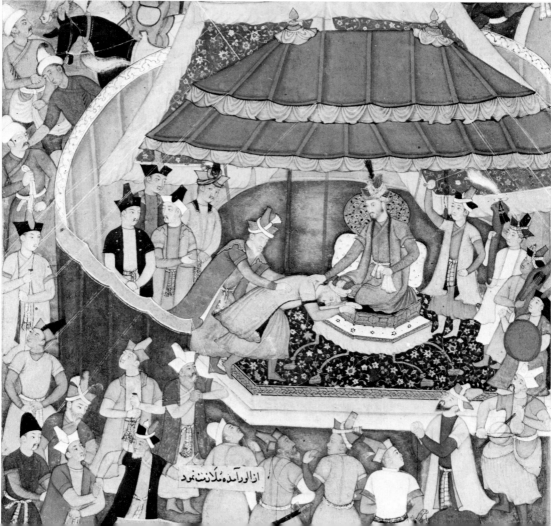

115 The library of Sher Shah's Purana Qila, Delhi, from which Humayun fell to his death after consulting his astrologers on the roof.

116 The white marble and red sandstone mausoleum raised for Humayun at Delhi by his widow took nine years to build, and ushered in the splendours of Moghul architecture.

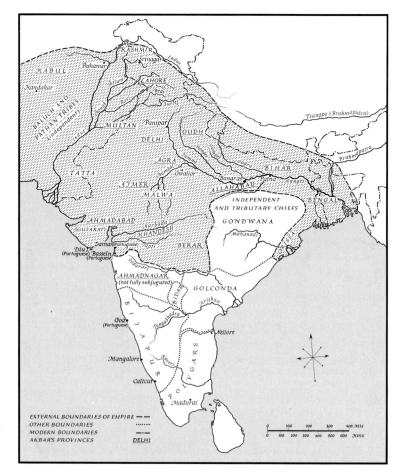

117 The extent of the Moghul Empire at the death of Akbar in 1605.

Note Based upon Survey of India map with the permission of the Surveyor General of India.
© Government of India copyright 1971.
The territorial waters of India extend into the sea to a distance of twelve nautical miles measured from the appropriate base line.

118 Akbar in his middle age, an intimate contemporary portrait. His great expansion of a shaky inheritance (right) was given by his large-minded statesmanship the character of an Indian empire, rather than an alien conquest.

The long reign of Akbar (1556–1605) saw the erection of an empire covering the whole of North India and part of the Deccan to the Godavari river, with a great north-western hump of hill country butting into Persia. Administrative devices were developed which retained much of their influence under later regimes; and the imperial concept was revived in a new form, recognized in India, admired in the outside world, and capable of projecting, even in its eventual dissolution, an ideal of unity.

Not yet fourteen at his accession, Akbar had first to defeat, in what is usually called the second battle of Panipat (1556), the army of Himu, a Hindu minister of the Afghan regime in Bengal and Bihar, who had proclaimed himself raja at Delhi before the young prince and his faithful Turcoman guardian, Bairam Khan, could get there. For the next four years the reins of government were in Bairam Khan's capable hands; and Akbar, before fully taking over, had to eliminate a palace conspiracy led by his foster-brother Adham Khan, whom he felled with his own hands when he attempted assassination.

Physical vitality contributed to Akbar's personal ascendancy as it had done to that of Babur. He could ride 240 miles in twenty-four

119 The young Emperor Akbar watches Adham Khan, who had assassinated his Prime Minister and tried to assassinate him, flung from a terrace in his palace at Agra in 1561.

hours to surprise and defeat a rebellion, and Malwa was annexed in 1562 after the Governor's force had been subdued by the Emperor's lightning attack with only three hundred horsemen. In the same year Akbar sealed his relations with Amber (later Jaipur) – the Rajput state which, as the nearest to Delhi and Agra, had recognized the imperial authority – by taking in marriage the Raja's daughter, who became the mother of his successor Jahangir. Towards a more general conciliation of his Hindu subjects he next abolished the pilgrim-tax and the *jizya*, the hated poll-tax on non-Muslims. Muslim nobles who objected to this trend had to be firmly subdued, and there were Rajputs who were not to be attached without a taste of force. The famous fortress of Chitor suffered a terrible siege, led by the Emperor, which ended with the ritual holocaust of high-caste women and the suicidal sally of its remaining defenders. The surrender of Ranthambor was negotiated under duress, on terms that secured symbolic dignities for its succession of chieftains. Other Rajput families followed the example of Raja Bhagwan Das of Amber, providing Akbar with generals, councillors and provincial governors, and sometimes with ladies for the imperial *zenana*.

113

The Emperor's revenue minister, Raja Todar Mall, was also a Hindu, though not a Rajput. He was the chief and able agent of a new system which (despite the complications which in the end let in the abuses it was designed to prevent) was somewhat fairer to the peasants – and more predictable in its application – than the extortions they had previously suffered. The 'king's share' of the land produce or its value, which had often been (and still was in the Deccan) as high as one-half, was now fixed at one-third. In Rajputana the feudal pattern remained, the king's share going to the rajas, who administered their states and paid a settled tribute to the Emperor. In the directly controlled provinces, however, Akbar treated his officers as a graded service, titled and privileged but paid in cash on rotating appointments. With the hereditary element of ambition abolished, the insecurity of tenure was compensated by salaries that were very large, even after taking into account the upkeep of horsemen – five thousand in the top grade – that these *mansabdars* commanded.

120 Akbar directing the building of Fatehpur Sikri. The new city, described by the English traveller Ralph Fitch as larger than the London of that time, was abandoned in Akbar's lifetime.

The system expanded with the empire which Akbar was building by conquest and cementing by policy and personal force. The flanking powers of Gujarat and Bengal were added in 1573 and 1576, Kashmir after another decade, Sind and the Baluchistan salient between 1591 and 1595. The northern dominion having been consolidated, the logic of Moghul pretensions dictated advance towards the South, where in the first part of Akbar's reign Vijayanagar had been eclipsed in the annihilating battle of Talikota (1565). The last Hindu empire had fallen to a combination of the Muslim states of the Deccan, which thereafter resumed their internecine conflicts. Intervening in these in his latter years, the Emperor secured supremacy over Berar, and incomplete control over Ahmadnagar.

Akbar's broad religious outlook developed from the mystical bent which had been shown in 1570, his twenty-eighth year, when he undertook the building of his new city of Fatehpur Sikri, in honour of a Sufi saint whose promise of a son for the dynasty had come to pass.

121 Fatehpur Sikri. In the centre is the Jodh Bai palace, named after one of Akbar's wives (a Rajput princess); beyond, the domes of the mosque at the tomb of the saint Shaik Salim Chisti; far left, the top of the huge Victory Gate.

This palatial wonder, twenty-six miles from Agra, was inhabited for only fourteen years, when the failure of its water-supply (it is thought) caused it to be abandoned. It was here that the Emperor assembled scholars of the Muslim and Hindu sects, Jains, Zoroastrians and Jesuits from Goa. What he caused to emerge from their debates was what he himself desired, not the victory of any one belief but a syncretic *Din-i-Illai* (Divine Faith) for the propagation of which he boldly declared his own infallibility. It was an astonishing enterprise, at once the result and the inspiration of his basic policy. 'For an empire ruled by one head,' he said in his statement of the new theology, 'it is a bad thing to have the members divided among themselves and at variance with one another.' As a religious experiment it marked Akbar as a heretic, antagonized the Ulema (see p. 100), disappointed the Jesuit hopes of a prize convert, and – though Jahangir continued the policy of toleration in the next reign – made no effective headway on its own account. But Akbar's memory is honoured for the attempt, for his concept of an India potentially greater than the sum of its parts, and for what his effort and example did achieve in the way of an upper-class cultural fusion, widely spread by the dispersal of a patrician civil service.

Under the Emperor's liberal patronage of Indian artists the art of the miniature, for which Humayun had imported Persian masters, evolved the Moghul blend which reached perfection at the court of Jahangir and was variously disseminated to subordinate centres, Muslim and

122 Below: Jahangir with a portrait of his father Akbar, who holds a globe of dominion.

Hindu – the native tradition contributing fresh colour, abundant themes and a realism which broke through Islamic convention in a florescence of portraiture. According to Abul Fazl, Akbar's distinguished annalist, minister and friend, more than a hundred workshops were established for the crafts and for making arms, armour and ordnance, in all of which the Emperor took a close and practical interest. Music, in which he delighted, furnished another medium of Hindu-Muslim intercourse, later to be interrupted but not destroyed by Aurangzeb's religious ban. His library of finely illustrated manuscripts was as celebrated as his gigantic animal-hunts, and the testimony to his intellectual curiosity is the more striking for the fact that he was illiterate. So said his son Jahangir, adding that 'no one could have guessed it'.

Neither Jahangir (1605–27) nor Shah Jahan (1627–58) came near to matching Akbar in character. The personality of Jahangir, who as Prince Salim had escaped by his father's clemency from the consequences of rebellion, was an unstable compound of vicious cruelty with the sensibilities of a poet and a connoisseur, of drunkenness and childish cupidity with subtlety, good humour and a marked attachment, in a polygamous setting, to his wife Nur Jahan. Shah Jahan waded to his throne through the blood of his male relatives, and finally abandoned it in a sensual decline; but left India one of its cherished romances: the old Emperor, interned in his own palace-fort at Agra, gazing at the Taj Mahal which he had created as the mausoleum of his wife Mumtaz.

123, 124 Shah Jahan (opposite), greatest of the Moghul builders, established at Delhi the new city of Shahjahanabad, with its vast Friday Mosque (see ill. 167) and palace, and at Agra rebuilt the city and palace, adding the world-famous Taj Mahal (below).

Both these Moghuls, however, showed just enough skill and firmness to preserve and slightly extend the empire left by Akbar. They shared as patrons in the climax of Indo-Persian culture, and in the creation of exquisite gardens in the Vale of Kashmir. That wealth and power could make an earthly paradise even in the scorching plains is the message of a couplet carved in one of the audience-halls of the Red Fort in Shahjahanabad, the new (but now called Old) Delhi founded by Shah Jahan on the bank of the Jumna; and in the same city this most prolific of builders raised one of Islam's greatest mosques. Projects on this scale clogged the normal flow of trade, and the tombs with which provincial nobles strove to emulate the imperial example were infructuous uses of accumulated capital. One of the worst of the recurrent famines, against which the peasant had no chance to protect himself, devastated most of North India from 1630 to 1632, while the Taj Mahal was in course of completion. For the peaceful latter half of Shah Jahan's reign the evidence nevertheless suggests a rural standard of living no worse, and perhaps somewhat better, than in Europe during the same period.

THE NEW ARRIVALS

The Dutch and the English had similar national, religious and economic motives for challenging the monopolistic Iberian power – as it became for sixty years with the union of Spain and Portugal under one crown in 1580. The Dutch were from the outset the more aggressive competitors for the trade of the spice-islands. Possession of the Antwerp exchange market, and a profitable trial voyage to the Indies, enabled them to jump the price of pepper, and it was this which in 1599 brought eighty London merchants together to form the East India Company. It was chartered by Queen Elizabeth I, Akbar's contemporary, on the last day of 1600.

This was a strictly commercial venture to the islands beyond India at which Drake had touched in his circumnavigation, and state protection was limited by a cautious foreign policy. The United East India Company of the Netherlands, on the other hand, was from its start in 1602 closely integrated with the state, charged with the positive aim of supplanting the Portuguese in the eastern seas, provided with heavily armed ships for the purpose and with ten times the capital of the English Company. In 1623, after two decades of rivalry between these nominal allies, a climax was reached at Amboyna in the Moluccas, one of the bases taken by the Dutch from the Portuguese. The English factors at this post were cruelly done to death by the Dutch on a trumped-up charge, with the important consequence that the concentration of the English Company's efforts was shifted from the archipelago to the Indian subcontinent.

Here they had by this time a foothold in the Gujarat port of Surat, within the Moghul Empire, with a subsidiary station on the eastern coast at Masulipatam, in Golconda territory. The need for such posts had become apparent with the perhaps predictable discovery that Indian cottons and calicoes were in better demand in the tropical islands than the woollen broadcloths that bulked so hopefully – along with iron,

125 Opposite, above left: a European of the late sixteenth century, seen by an Indian artist. He leaves his native landscape behind him and faces an Indian scene

126 Opposite, above right: part of the list of subscriptions promised for the first voyage of the East India Company, dated 22 September 1599. At the top of the list is the Lord Mayor of London, who subscribed £200.

127 Opposite, below: a European mercantile 'factory' in 1665. The Dutch establishment on the Hooghly, with warehouses, offices, residences and gardens within an enclave. The English settlement further downstream, which was to become Calcutta, was founded in 1690.

tin, lead and mercury – in the first outward cargoes from London. But the Portuguese, whose command of the 'country trade' and its ramifications within the zone had been of greater value than commerce with Europe, were still to be reckoned with in the Arabian Sea. 'Golden Goa' proclaimed their accumulated wealth and harboured their naval strength and reputation, and the Jesuit Fathers formed a political clique at the court of Jahangir.

The Dutch inroads upon this pride and power were not displeasing in Moghul eyes; but it had taken the English – arriving at Surat in 1608, as one of the Portuguese captains sneered, from 'an island of no import' – ten difficult years to confirm their 'factory', or warehouse and settlement, with the necessary rights. Mere merchants were generally beneath the Moghul notice, and Jahangir's reception of William Hawkins, leader of the third English voyage, veered from surprising geniality to frustrating coolness. Even the efforts of a royally accredited envoy, the famous Sir Thomas Roe, would hardly have produced results without the engagements in which English sea-captains, against great odds and often in disregard of their distant sovereign's policy, had at the same time destroyed the legend of Portuguese invincibility in the Indian waters. When a harder Moghul line towards aliens and infidels came in with Shah Jahan, it was the Portuguese who were made to feel it, in the violent extirpation of their Bengal post.

Sir Thomas Roe has often been quoted for his advice to the East India Company:

> A war and traffic are incompatible. By my consent, ye shall no way engage yourselves but at sea, where you are like to gain as often as to lose. It is the beggaring of the Portugal. . . . It hath been also the error of the Dutch, who seek plantation here by the sword. . . . Let this be received as a rule, that, if you will profit, seek it at sea, and in quiet trade; for without controversy it is an error to affect garrisons and land wars in India.

The English were in no position to ignore this admonition, and in 1635 they reached an advantageous accord with Portuguese interests in the East. Trade then increased, and although the general situation of the Company remained precarious, it had founded by 1647 twenty-seven small Indian posts, chiefly though not exclusively at coastal points. Among these settlements was the harbourless stretch of Coromandel beach, first leased and later confirmed as an English holding by the last of the Vijayanagar dynasty, where the building of Fort St George in 1644 was the beginning of Madras. The Portuguese were close neighbours at San Thome, and the Danes had a concession from the Tanjore Raja further south, at Tranquebar in the Kaveri estuary. Between the two, at Pondicherry, the French in 1674 were the last to arrive, by which time the Dutch, having finally reduced the Portuguese power in the East Indies, had deprived them between 1656 and 1663 of Colombo in Ceylon and of their Malabar holdings. In 1665 the Portuguese Viceroy reluctantly handed over to the English the enclave of Bombay, with its fine harbour, which had been included five years earlier in the dowry of Catherine of Braganza on her marriage to Charles II. This

128 Sir Thomas Roe, who from 1615 to 1619 steered the first English merchant settlement through great difficulties to an acknowledged status.

was Crown property, leased to the Company from 1668, and shortly to succeed as headquarters the exposed settlement at Surat.

The English, after eighty years' experience in commercial, political and public relations in an alien and difficult environment, made one rash departure from the Roe principle. Prompted from London by a high-handed Company President, their Surat Council embroiled themselves, from 1685 to 1688, in a state of belligerence towards the Emperor Aurangzeb himself. Fortunately for them the Moghul, after a demonstration of strength, contented himself with the Company's apology. The Surat factory, which had been seized, was restored, and in Bengal the Company was allowed a new settlement, on condition of a return to respectful behaviour. This was the site which in 1696 became Fort William, and subsequently Calcutta.

AURANGZEB AND THE BREAK-UP OF THE MOGHUL EMPIRE

According to viewpoint the portrait of Aurangzeb (1658–1707) is that of a devout Sunni, selfless and iron-willed, or of a reckless bigot, his memorial the mosque that towered blatantly (until its collapse in 1949) over the holiest Hindu city of Banaras. What is beyond question is that his long and immensely active reign achieved the widest expansion of the Moghul Empire, and heralded its calamitous decline.

129 Aurangzeb's mosque at Banaras, dominating the sacred Hindu city, as it appeared in 1833.

Shah Jahan had moved in various ways to restrict Hindu activities and aspirations. Aurangzeb's attack upon the extravagance of the imperial court, his puritanical aversion to all the arts except that of Muslim calligraphy, and his iconoclastic zeal, would in themselves have damaged cultural harmony. But he also revived the tax on non-Muslims, sending in his armour – in this case elephants – when Hindus gathered to protest. Shah Jahan had stopped short of tampering with the Rajput alliance, but his son seemed prepared to dispense with these servants of the empire, and declined to exempt them from the tax. In the wasteful fighting that followed he brought the premier state of Mewar to some degree of submission in 1684, but in Marwar a state of warfare continued throughout his reign. Even Amber, loyal to the policy of association, had to suffer the destruction of temples. A reservoir of fighting men was closed to the Moghul, and a drain on Moghul forces opened.

For the virile Marathas, who emerged with apparent suddenness under the outstanding leadership of Shivaji (1627–80) the threat to Hindu institutions was an effective spur. Their homeland was the hard hill-country of the Western Ghats, and before Shivaji's bid for independent power they had been mercenaries and feudatories of the Bijapur sultans. Shudras with a tradition of peasant smallholding provided the fighting stock, brahmans the political skills. Towards the latter Shivaji, whose own origins were dubious, showed respect and great generosity, and the unity of purpose he inspired in the Marathas was unweakened by caste divisions. Even so, the brahmans needed much persuasion to invest him with the kshatriya pedigree and status required for kingship. An audacious exploit of 1664, Shivaji's first far-flung descent upon the Moghul port of Surat (which yielded rich plunder) had the side-effect of advancing the prestige of the English merchants, who stood alone in the successful defence of themselves and their factory. It further induced Aurangzeb to bring Shivaji into a tributary relationship, but though the Emperor drew 'the Grand Rebel' (as the English called him) into audience at Agra he failed to treat him, as Akbar would have done, as a ruling prince. Angrily refusing to offer submission, Shivaji outwitted by a daring escape the attempt to detain him in Agra. Returning to his own people to be crowned with significant pomp, he next showed his capacities in an expedition across the Deccan to the south-east coast at Tanjore, organizing his scattered conquests as he went. When he died in 1680 he had brought into being a Hindu raj with which the Muslim states of Bijapur and Golconda, long resistant to the Moghul power, were glad to ally themselves. Aurangzeb called him 'the Mountain Rat'. 'My armies have been employed against him for nineteen years,' he said, 'and nevertheless his state has always been increasing.'

The Maratha strength derived from extreme mobility from secure bases. Shivaji's fortresses were almost impregnable on their rugged peaks, and from the coastal strip below them he waged naval warfare against the Arab admirals in the imperial service. On land the zestful opportunism of hard-riding commando tactics and deceptive skills was

given, under his excellent discipline and with the fervour of a cause, the promise of something more substantial; and his treatment of prisoners, of women, and of the populations that he taxed and administered, was generally praised. After his death, however, the Marathas' militarism became increasingly predatory, and though they carried their presence and fame over immense distances, it was more often as a scourge than an inspiration. Individual leaders of ability were to appear in the succession states of their first empire, but it was only by their failure to achieve central power that the dream that they could have used it for India's good was able to survive.

Another reaction from Aurangzeb's implacable orthodoxy (painfully visited upon the sects of his own faith as well as upon non-Muslims) was the path to militant separatism taken by the Sikhs. The ninth Sikh Guru, Tegh Bahadur, summoned by the Emperor to Delhi, was tortured and beheaded when he refused to embrace Islam. After the death of Aurangzeb and the murder of the last Guru, a peasant rising in the Punjab under Sikh leadership was crushed in 1715 after initial successes, this time with several hundred executions to follow the familiarly scornful defiance of conversion. This was an eclipse, but in the nature of the Sikhs – and of eclipses – only temporary.

The map of an Islamic dominion that Aurangzeb finally drew left outside the empire only the lands of the Hindu Polygars at the tip of the peninsula, their Calicut dependency and the Portuguese enclave around Goa. But the effort, continued against the counsels of history and of his closest advisers, was self-defeating. In the first half of his reign his generals in the Deccan had been deprived of adequate forces by the ambitious imperial campaigns in the north-east, the north-west, and against the Rajputs, and this had a corrupting effect. In 1683, when Shivaji had been succeeded by a dissolute son, when the last strong

130 Landscape in the Western Ghats, which provided natural defences for Shivaji's Marathas, and bases for their operations by land and sea.

123

131 The indefatigable Aurangzeb, last of the great Moghuls, who enlarged the empire but treated it like a Muslim state.

member of Bijapur's Adil Shah dynasty had died and the Golconda Sultan was reported to be sunk in his pleasures, the Emperor moved south of the Narbada to take charge of operations, and he never came back. For the twenty-five years left to him the empire was ruled from his Deccan camp. With its rear headquarters at Ahmadnagar, it was described by an Italian witness as a moving city, thirty miles in circumference, containing half a million camp-followers besides the huge army whose annual losses (according to another writer) were computed at 100,000 men and more than 300,000 transport animals. The burden on a land where existing administrations had been shattered was disastrous, and in 1702–3 famine and plague killed more than two million in the Deccan. The Marathas, their discipline and cohesion broken by Aurangzeb's blows, could still harass the stricken countryside and the imperial army when it struggled back to Ahmadnagar with the Emperor, dying at last in his ninetieth year. In the North, where he had not been seen for a quarter of a century, rivals were in motion for the succession. As Muhammad bin Tughluq had found three and a half centuries earlier, the Deccan could not be conquered from the Gangetic plain, nor Hindustan controlled from the Deccan. The idea of an imperium was ahead of its communications.

Even in his longevity Aurangzeb contributed to the ultimate collapse, since it served to shorten to five years the reign of the ablest of his sons, Bahadur Shah (till then known as Shah Alam), who was sixty-three when he won the throne. After his death in 1712 a half-century of decay was shared between eight emperors, of whom three were murdered, one was deposed, and none was competent – or indeed much concerned – to arrest the process. In 1724 the Deccan province became effectively independent under its Moghul governor, Asaf Jah (Nizam-ul-Mulk), whose successors ruled as nizams of Hyderabad down to 1948. From Poona, Maratha policy was now controlled by brahman ministers (peshwas), and with the Nizam-ul-Mulk blocking expansion in the Deccan the Peshwa Baji Rao I – soldier as well as statesman – was looking northwards: so that by 1738 the Marathas had eliminated the Moghul power from Malwa, forcing the Emperor Muhammad Shah to a treaty by raiding to the outskirts of Delhi. This opened a corridor between Hindustan and the Deccan, through which their marauding horsemen could reach the coast of Orissa and Bengal. Kabul was lost to the empire in 1739, and Nadir Shah, a Persian of Turki origin, was provoked by procrastination and treachery into a descent through the Punjab in the old style and the destruction of a superior but planless Moghul army. After supervising a day-long butchery in the streets of Delhi, Nadir Shah stayed for a few months and then departed for Persia, loaded with a vast treasure that included the bejewelled Peacock Throne.

Sind and Gujarat ceased to be subordinate in 1750, Oudh and the Punjab in 1754. The viceroys and nawabs of Bengal continued to pay tribute, but acted without reference to Delhi, as in the case of Nawab Siraj-ad-daula's momentous assault on the English in Fort William in 1756. Early in 1757 Delhi was again sacked, and Mathura put to fire and sword, this time by the formidable Afghan Ahmad Shah Abdali. The Marathas, called in as rescuers, saw the prize of central power nearing their own grasp when they drove the Afghans back into the Punjab. But Ahmad Shah Abdali advanced again in 1761, out-manœuvred the Marathas, and brought them to decisive battle on the ground of his own choice, which was once more at Panipat. The charge of thirteen thousand Maratha horsemen, with their old Hindu war-cry, was answered by an Afghan counter-attack which destroyed them almost to a man, strewing them over the field 'like mown tulips'. For ten years thereafter the Marathas disappeared from the northern scene; but the Afghan victor was robbed of the fruits by the disaffection of his men and had to withdraw to the north-west, where he did not live to make another attempt. The two effective contenders for the still prestigious centre being thus neutralized, the 'Forty Years' Anarchy' opened at the moment when the East India Company had been brought by Clive and circumstance to a new and unexpected role.

THE ANGLO-FRENCH INVOLVEMENT

The collapse of the Moghul system provided the power vacuum which the British were eventually to fill. But it was the French in India who seized the political initiative and had to be fought for the decision, and the defining event was the war which opened in Europe in 1744 over the Austrian, not the Moghul succession.

After 150 years of minding its own business the East India Company had a stake of great proportions to protect. Its earnings were made up by the carrying and 'country' trade, the entrepôt commerce with China, and the profit on European sales of Eastern goods; for the direct trade with India had always shown an adverse balance, with a drain of bullion to the East which English mercantile economists viewed, then and later, with a rooted misgiving. The urban growth of the Company's three chief centres on the Indian coasts, under a stated policy of encouraging 'merchants of all nations and conditions to trust their estates and families and ships there', increasingly demanded the security of fortification, a defensive militia (the first 'sepoys') and the ability to land sailors or soldiers in an emergency. The development of Bombay was delayed by internal dissension as well as Maratha encirclement, but Madras was now a populous cosmopolitan city, protected and governed from Fort St George under settlements requiring the English (and their French neighbours at Pondicherry) to cultivate the favour of the Moghul Nawab of the Carnatic. In Bengal, with another nawab to be watched, Calcutta was the more recent growth, at a deep-water anchorage more than eighty miles up the Hooghly but downstream from the French settlement at Chandernagar. The town was still much smaller than Madras, but its lower living-costs and better opportunities for private trade fed the dreams of young and wretchedly paid Company 'writers' at the southern post, among whom, from 1744, was Robert Clive. Joseph François Dupleix had been governor of Pondicherry since 1742.

Unlike the East India Company, which was autonomous but expected to provide state funds in return for its charters, the French

132 Robert, Lord Clive, whose boldness and skill turned the English mercantile establishment into a military power.

Compagnie des Indes was a political instrument, depending on the home government for its direction and for a substantial part of its finance. In its first thirty years French commercial competition had given the well-established English no cause for concern, and their local relations had been reasonably neutral even when their home countries had been opposed in war. By 1744, however, France's Indian Ocean trade had developed such a rate of expansion that the chance of eliminating it provided by war in Europe was not one to be overlooked.

In fact the initiative had already been taken by Dupleix. His secret engagements with the Nawab of the Carnatic (which he subsequently broke) began that web of involvement with competing Indian ambitions, based on the exchange value of Western military skills, in which Clive was to learn from the French example. The fact that Dupleix was the first to receive naval reinforcements (from Mauritius) emphasized an element in which the British were to triumph, but which in this instance helped the French to capture Madras and its government at a stroke. Two years later (1748) Madras was restored by the peace-treaty made in Europe; but in the same year the death of the veteran Nizam-ul-Mulk produced in Hyderabad and its Carnatic dependency a situation made for Dupleix's manipulating genius and for his now unemployed troops under the Marquis de Bussy. Hyderabad was secured for a French-supported candidate, but in the struggle of rival contenders for the Carnatic the tide was turned by Clive. He had escaped from the Madras débâcle, transferred to the Company's military service, and now leaped into fame with such spectacular exploits as the capture and defence of Arcot. The French and their allies were brought to surrender, the English client Muhammad Ali entered upon a long but hardly glorious career as Nawab of the Carnatic, and Dupleix was recalled in disgrace.

In Europe a realignment of allies (but with Britain and France still opposed) produced in August 1756 the clash that became the Seven Years War. In India the area of decision changed in the same summer to Bengal, where the young Nawab Siraj-ud-daula, finding the English in Fort William truculent, asserted himself in overwhelming force and with French and Turkish gunners. The hopeless defence of the English enclave, led by those few members of the Calcutta Council who had not fled downstream with the non-combatants, ended in the ordeal of a hideous night's confinement in the fort's lock-up – the 'Black Hole of Calcutta' as it became in the folklore of a later generation – from which only a handful survived. That the East India Company itself survived as a hinge of history was due to sea communications and to Clive, who arrived in the Hooghly with Admiral Watson's fleet and a contingent of royal troops – among the first to be sent to India and now riskily diverted from the south. Reversal of the Calcutta disaster was followed by the reduction of French Chandernagar and then, on 23 June 1757, by the extraordinary victory of Plassey.

Plassey deserves its fame, but not as a feat of arms. It was the turning-point of a political conspiracy, begun by Hindu financiers and forwarded with nerve and skill by Clive, to replace the Nawab by one of

133 Nawab Muhammad Ali of the Carnatic, who owed his position to the British but bequeathed them astronomical debts.

134 Clive's confidential agent, Watts, in the negotiations with Mir Jafar (standing at the far left) that facilitated the British victory at Plassey.

his nobles, Mir Jafar. With everything to lose and against numerical odds of sixteen to one, Clive gambled on the defection from the Nawab's army of the force commanded by Mir Jafar, who had not yet declared himself, even in secret. At the climax of this rain-drenched engagement Mir Jafar kept his men out of action and in the result became nawab, outwardly supreme in Bengal and Bihar but a puppet of Clive (whose reward was £234,000 and an estate worth £30,000 a year) and of the Calcutta Council. The Council's immediate pickings, though considerable, were less than exaggerated estimates of the late Nawab's treasury had led them to expect, but the situation allowed the merchants and their agents a field for irresponsible rapacity which, with Clive's departure for England in 1760, lost the relative restraints which he had imposed. In his absence Mir Jafar was replaced by Mir Kasim, who also gave trouble, so that Mir Jafar was restored, each change being accompanied with substantial payments to the Council. A great and populous province was being bled to death.

On the eve of his sailing Clive had learnt of the defeat of the French in the Carnatic by Eyre Coote; and shortly before his return to Bengal another able officer, Hector Munro, added military meaning to the result of Plassey by routing at Buxar in Bihar (1764) an imperial and confederate army of six times his own strength. The defeated Emperor, Shah Alam II, sent Munro his congratulations and proposed an alliance. On the reappearance of Baron Clive of Plassey (as he had now become) for a second spell as governor at Calcutta – and with enlarged powers to control the chaos – what was needed was a decision on the terms of the Company's revolutionized existence. In reaching this Clive allowed Oudh, whose ruler had involved the Emperor in the contest with the English, to become a buffer state, attached to the Company by its own interests. For the Emperor, now made homeless by the Afghans, a tract was provided around Allahabad. The East India Company, by the imperial grant of the *Diwani*, or revenue function, of Bengal, Bihar and Orissa, received legal recognition as an Indian potentate. Clive's preference, however, was for a dual system of control, leaving the administration of the Diwani to the officials of the Nawab. This fictional device was not to last beyond 1772, when Warren Hastings was charged from London to conclude it.

CHAPTER EIGHT

The British Period

THE PATH TO PARAMOUNTCY

For the East India Company the transition from 'quiet trade' to the mastery of a rich province presented the painful paradox of near-bankruptcy. While their servants were returning with scandalously acquired wealth, the directors, baulked by maladministration of a revenue surplus to take care of the annual investment, had to turn to the Government (having been refused by the City) for a large loan. This led to the first steps, in the Regulating Act of 1773, towards parliamentary supervision of the Company's affairs. The actions and personalities of the British-Indian stage being thus drawn into the factious politics of Westminster, there ascended from that dubious arena important enunciations of political idealism. The unworthy episode of the impeachment of Warren Hastings, which dragged on for seven years before his name was cleared, was at the same time the means by which Edmund Burke's theories of trusteeship entered the public consciousness and the field of policy.

Calcutta, however, was distant from London by six months' sail. During the half-century that followed Clive's final departure, the enlargement of British power which hindsight tends to mistake for destiny stemmed from the reactions of men on the spot to the shifting pressures of other contestants. Warren Hastings, governor in Bengal from 1772, and from 1774 to 1778 the first governor-general, accepted his task as a holding operation. 'The dominion of all India', he wrote, 'is what I never wish to see.' Within that charge he was expected to conjure, out of the chaos which had returned on Clive's departure, not simply order but profitable order – a restoration of revenue and commerce without the drain of land wars and costly administration against which Roe had long ago warned. He found a starting-point in the defection of the Emperor Shah Alam II into the protection of the Marathas, who now loomed again as a loose confederacy : Sindhia and Holkar in the north, the Gaikwar in the east, the Bhonsla in the west and the Peshwa in Maharashtra. This enabled Warren Hastings to discontinue the tribute to the imperial treasury, and to sell to the Nawab of Oudh the lands assigned to Shah Alam by Clive. By next hiring Company troops to Oudh so that its Nawab could overrun his Rohilla neighbours – peaceable Afghan settlers – Hastings began the 'subsidiary system' which exposed him to the charge of involving his nation in the aggressions and oppressions of Indian despots.

135 Opposite: the east front of Government House, Calcutta, built in 1798–1803 for Governor-General Lord Wellesley, whose recall was partly due to the extravagant outlay.

136 Warren Hastings, the great consolidator of the British position and first governor-general, painted in India by Tilly Kettle.

137 The splendours of the British Residency in Hyderabad asserted the power of the Company in the Nizam's dominions under the subsidiary system.

Morality apart, the practical statesmanship of stabilizing the Company's frontier in the north-west was soon evident. Inept provocations by the governments of Bombay and of Madras had the effect by 1780 of confronting the Governor-General with a hostile coalition of the main Indian powers: the Maratha Confederacy, the Nizam of Hyderabad and – operating from the Mysore plateau – the formidable Haidar Ali. It was an extreme situation at a time when Britain was hard pressed in Europe and a French fleet again made a menacing appearance (in fact its last) in the Bay of Bengal. With extraordinary resolution Hastings rescued first Bombay and then Madras by military expeditions, and by diplomatic finesse detached one by one the foremost Maratha chief Sindhia, the Nizam in the centre, and also the Peshwa. The Indian contenders never again achieved this unity. But in the South, where Haidar Ali was succeeded in 1782 by his son Tipu Sultan – the Tiger of Mysore, or *citoyen Tipu* as he was called from his connivance with Napoleon – two more wars were to be fought before security for Madras was translated into supremacy. One was conducted by Lord Cornwallis, governor-general from 1786 to 1798 and at the same time commander-in-chief; the other, ending with the death of Tipu in the storming of Seringapatam in 1799, was in the term of Lord Wellesley, who had the services of his brother Arthur, the future Duke of Wellington.

SULTANO TIPPOO DEVICTO OBSIDES RECIPIT MDCCXCII.

Lord Wellesley (1798–1805) was a 'sacred trust' imperialist, convinced that 'no greater blessing can be conferred on the native inhabitants of India than the extension of British authority'. Successful campaigns gained territorial continuity down the eastern coast and across the southern peninsula; French influence at the Nizam's court was eliminated in a subsidiary alliance, and the same course was pursued with a restored Hindu Mysore and with the Peshwa Bhaji Rao II, who fled to British protection from his rival Holkar. This intrusion upon the Maratha Confederacy brought the Sindhia and Bhonsla rulers to the offensive, to be defeated in brilliant and hard-fought campaigns by General Lake in the North and Arthur (now Major-General) Wellesley in the Deccan. In the meantime Ceylon, following the French occupation of Holland, had passed from Dutch to British hands to become a separate Crown Colony. But although Wellesley regarded his forward policy in India as an extension of the struggle with Napoleon in Europe and the eastern Mediterranean, the Company and its shareholders were aghast at its expense and at symptoms of grandeur such as Calcutta's vast new Government House. The younger Pitt's historic India Act of 1784, moreover, had declared territorial expansion in India to be 'repugnant to the wish, the honour and policy of this nation'. In 1805, the year of Trafalgar, Wellesley was recalled.

138 Lord Cornwallis receiving the two sons of Tipu Sultan as hostages after the First Mysore War.

139 Colonel James Skinner (seated, with one of his sons) holding a durbar for his 'free regiment' of horse at Hansi, north of Delhi.

Lake's destruction of Sindhia's great Army of Hindustan, trained and led mainly by outstanding French officers, brought to a close the colourful age of the freelances, in which adventurers from several European countries had served their Maratha paymasters or sometimes, like the Irishman 'King' Thomas, carved out fiefs for themselves; and Wellesley had ensured success by drawing away those British mercenaries with their forces who had not been killed by their employers when hostilities opened (the famous Eurasian Colonel Skinner was one of his catches). Victory also secured for the British the city and district of Delhi, with the old Emperor, blinded by the Afghans and rescued by Sindhia, and now commonly called the King of Delhi. The Marathas had not been finally crushed, but Wellesley's subsidiary system, developing for expansion the model originated by Warren Hastings for defence, had set the pattern which, with a final total of 562 Indian states, mostly tiny but a few very large, was to be a condition of empire and a problem for its devolution.

The Earl of Moira – more generally, if confusingly, known as Marquess of Hastings – began his eventful decade of office in 1813. He was greatly served by men of the calibre of Mountstuart Elphinstone, Sir John Malcolm, Sir Charles Metcalfe and Sir Thomas Munro, and he himself saw through the rapidly expanded British system to the strains and estrangements it had created. Events, however, left him no choice but vigorous measures. On the northern mountain flank the Gurkhas of Nepal inflicted military disasters before the lessons were learnt and the Himalayan kingdom brought to a settlement (1813) based on mutual respect, and gaining for the British a staunch ally, a recruiting-ground of incomparable mercenaries, and a wedge of territory (Kumaon and Garwhal) up to the high watershed. Westwards lay the growing Sikh empire of Ranjit Singh (1780–1839) with whom a wary friend-ship was established. The full-scale operations, in part conducted by Lord Hastings himself, required to eliminate the Pindaris – sweepings of the wars in Central and Northern India who preyed savagely on defenceless populations – moved as expected into the last Maratha War of 1817–19. Sindhia and Holkar, by now regimes of pillage, were finally broken, and the unlamented Peshwa deposed, his lands being annexed to Bombay. The Gaikwar's more orderly state received pro-tection, as did the Rajput princes who had been clamouring for it. From southernmost Cape Comorin to the eastern borders of Sind and the Punjab, this was paramountcy.

Burmese aggressions in the regions from Assam to the Arakan provoked the First Burma War of 1824–6, which secured the eastern border. The more controversial process of advance in the north-west was not initiated until 1839, when the death of Ranjit Singh produced an imbalance in which fears of the rising tide of Russian power in

140 Lord Moira, Marquess of Hastings, and his wife at a Luck-now banquet given in 1814 by Nawab Ghazi-ud-din Haidar of Oudh after he had been granted the title of king by the British.

141 A bazaar-quarter in Sind-hia's camp, at a time (1809) when the Maratha chiefs were fighting among themselves. They were finally subdued in the Third Maratha War, 1817–19, which pacified Central India and decided the British supremacy.

Central Asia led under Lord Auckland (1836–42) to ill-conceived intervention in Afghanistan. The catastrophe from which a lone survivor rode back through the Khyber to tell of the fate of an army of sixteen thousand was a blow to prestige which the next governor-general, Lord Ellenborough (recalled in 1844) sought to mend by the conquest of Sind: an operation described in advance by its executant, Sir Charles Napier, as 'a very advantageous, useful, humane piece of rascality'. For the two bloodily contested Sikh Wars of 1845–6 and 1848–9, on the other hand, there was direct provocation in the Sikh advance across the Sutlej into British-protected territory. The Punjab of the great Ranjit Singh passed from the hands of his lawless successors into those which could convert it, in the phase made famous by Henry and John Lawrence and their assistants, into a largely reconciled British province. Kashmir, which by now had a predominantly Muslim population, had been part of Ranjit Singh's empire; and it was not in that sense incongruous (though fraught with later consequence for India and Pakistan) to transfer it as a British subsidiary to a Dogra (Hindu) raja and his line.

Behind the dedicated individualism of the 'Punjab system' was the energy of a governor-general, Lord Dalhousie (1848–56), self-called 'a curious compound of despot and radical', who proceeded to tidy up the map of paramountcy in the interest of efficiency and material progress. The doctrine of 'lapse', attached to the prerogative by which accession was recognized in a subsidiary state, was used for the annexa-tion of a number of territories by disallowing the adoption of an heir, though valid by Hindu law where there was no natural succession. In

the case of the Muslim King of Oudh, as the Company had titled him, a different pretext was found in gross misrule. This had been a barely tolerated scandal over several reigns, but in 1856 it was dealt with by annexation. Hindu and Muslim princes alike had thus been given cause for apprehension and resentment.

142 *Bolan Pass*, an anonymous commentary on the extinction of a British-Indian army in the futile disaster of the First Afghan War.

REFORM AND REVOLT

The guidelines of Pitt's 1784 Act endured, with progressive adjustments, until the formal supersession of Company by Crown in 1858. Up to 1833 the Company continued its commercial existence, though its monopoly had been confined from 1813 to the trade with China and in tea. While its servants were being turned into administrators it retained, until the change to recruitment by open competition in 1853, its patronage of appointments; but over all its non-commercial activities the ultimate control rested with a Board responsible to the Government, and thereby to Parliament.

The pattern of the service in India had been set by Cornwallis, armed by Pitt's Act with the powers that Warren Hastings had lacked in his drive for an orderly system. The power to increase the pay of officials on a substantial scale, for instance, was necessary for the enforcement of regulations prohibiting the private trading with which they had hitherto been allowed to compensate for minimal salaries. Under the lofty integrity of Cornwallis, however, corruption was stamped out, as Percival Spear observed in his key-work on *The Nabobs*, 'at the cost of equality and co-operation'. The exclusion of Indians from all the higher posts of the new administration seems to

135

143, 144 Right and opposite: cross-currents of fashion. An Indian ruler in British uniform, by a Jaipur artist (*c.* 1860), and an Englishman of about 1770–90 in Lucknow, in Indian dress and smoking a hookah.

have been based on the view that their malpractices were beyond the vigilance that could be applied to British officials. The mistrust that it expressed, and the social estrangement to which it contributed, were a departure from the temper of Warren Hastings and his regime, in which upper-class contacts had had the ease of a genuine racial equality, and the enthusiastic labours of scholars and translators had bred a cultivated respect for the country and its people.

From the best and most experienced Company servants there was outspoken criticism of this injection of mistrust, of the neglect of valuable native talents and of the tendency to increase by unemployment the very defects that were alleged. Of the Westernizing 'innovations' which Malcolm and Munro both regarded as a disastrous impertinence, the first had been the establishment, as early as 1773, of a Supreme Court in Calcutta, conducted by Crown-appointed judges from England, and followed by similar urban jurisdictions in Madras and Bombay. Intended to protect Indians by controlling Europeans, these did assert equality before the law, but their concepts and procedures were bewilderingly alien. The rule of law in supersession of anarchy was more apparent in the countryside, in the personal government of the district officer as collector and magistrate. It was the ideas and first researches of Warren Hastings that slowly triumphed in the recognition of caste and other customary laws, and some of the Muslim criminal law; and the great work of forming the Penal Code, for

145 Raja Ram Mohun Roy, the brilliant Hindu reformer who promoted acceptance of the English language as a vehicle of Western thought and knowledge for the future benefit of India.

which T.B. Macaulay was sent out as Law Member of the Council under the Charter Act of 1833, was aimed in his own words at establishing 'uniformity where you can have it, diversity where you must have it, but in all cases certainty'.

Acquiescence in British rule was itself a condition of the force behind it, since the military instrument was so largely Indian in its composition; and the avoidance of any interference with religion, which had begun as a mercantile principle, was continued as an essential of government by a foreign minority. It was the exclusion of Christian missionaries from British India which compelled the Baptist William Carey – whose educational operations stimulated the printing of Indian languages – to work from the Danish settlement of Serampore. The first licensing of Christian missionaries was secured in 1813, under pressure from the powerful Evangelical movement in England, which had introduced into the consciousness of political mission inspired by Burke a growing sense of spiritual obligation towards the populations committed by Providence into Britain's charge. At the same time the Hindu reform movement in Bengal, under the brilliant leadership of Raja Ram Mohun Roy (1770–1833) facilitated British-Indian intercourse in the pursuit of enlightenment while purifying and strengthening Hinduism to meet the challenge of assumed superiority in Western religion. The 'Father of Modern India', as Roy has since been called by his countrymen, had studied the theologies of Hinduism,

137

Buddhism, Islam, Judaism and Christianity in their source-languages. He was the founder of secondary schools, of the first purely Indian newspapers, and of the Brahmo Samaj for theistic and ethical reform, carried further after his death by Debendranath Tagore and Keshub Chunder Sen. His journey to England, where he was received with honour and attention, was itself a defiance of Hindu orthodoxy, and enabled him to present an Indian case for the suppression of suttee, as against a brahman petition to the Privy Council urging non-interference. He died in England, but not before his influence had encouraged the liberal-minded Governor-General Lord William Bentinck to proceed in 1829 to the legal abolition of widow-burning in British India. This was a test case for the interference principle, and though its full effect was not immediate, neither was there violent reaction. The bands of robber-stranglers called Thugs, against whom Bentinck moved with a prolonged and difficult police-operation conducted by Sir William Sleeman, also claimed ritual sanctions, but with less support from public opinion.

The most fateful decision of Bentinck's term (1828–35) was that which in his last year channelled the official education policy, first sanctioned in 1813, towards 'imparting to the Native population knowledge of English literature and science through the medium of the English language'. Victory over the 'orientalists', who wanted the

146 Veterans of the four thousand 'Thugs' captured by Sleeman in his diligent extirpation of the killer bands, photographed in jail where they had been put to carpet-making and were visited by travellers. About four hundred had been executed after scrupulous presentation of evidence.

available funds to be used in continuance of the Warren Hastings policy of patronizing Persian, Arabic and Sanskrit studies, was clinched by Macaulay in the famous Minute which argued that 'a single shelf of a good European library is worth the whole native literature of India and Arabia'. Though his eloquence derived from ignorance of what he was denigrating, his cause answered the modernizing aspirations of the Ram Mohun Roy persuasion, who shared Bentinck's belief in the English language as 'the key to all improvements'. An important step taken at the same time was the replacement of Persian by English as the official language and in the higher law-courts, and by regional languages in the lower courts.

The new educational policy, limited to the higher level by finance but hopefully systematized from 1854, was separately conducted in the three Presidencies. If it did not fulfil Macaulay's forecast of a transforming downward 'filtration' of Western knowledge and ideas, it carried a threat to the old order as clear as the gun-salute from Fort William which in 1836 honoured the first Hindu student to defy orthodoxy by performing a dissection in the new Calcutta Medical College. And when Dalhousie took over in 1848, the programme was promoted with the zeal for Westernizing progress which marked all his activities, shortening his life by the effort and sowing among his seminal measures the tares of revolt.

147 Model in painted wood of a *cutcherry*, or court, presided over by an official of the East India Company.

148, 149 Indian lithographs of a train carrying Indian ladies and a European, with a Sikh signalman (above), and railway-surveying in the Punjab (right). As a threat to established ways, the new communications contributed to the fears and resentments that exploded in 1857.

Communications were foremost in Dalhousie's utilitarian plan. New and much improved roads, the first three hundred miles of railway construction, connection of the chief centres by telegraph, a cheap and efficient postal service, brought measurable benefits to all who were prepared to take advantage of the acceleration of trade and information. But there was a wide disturbance of conservative minds, besides the new and painful adjustments demanded in the contact of castes and the breakdown of communities. The works that raised no such difficulties were in irrigation. Under Lord Hastings the renewal of the Moghul canal system in the Delhi region, which had decayed during the northern wars, had had an excellent effect; and improvements had begun also in the South, where tank-reservoirs attested the exemplary care of ancient dynasties. The chief enterprise of Dalhousie's term was the completion to 450 miles of the Ganges Canal and its outworks, but at the time of the 1857 Mutiny, when he had been succeeded by Canning (1856–62), the attack on famine was as yet a promise.

Nearly forty years earlier Elphinstone, whose great work in Bombay and Maharashtra was animated by the belief that British rule must be short-lived, had spoken of the sepoy army as 'a delicate and dangerous machine, which a little mismanagement may easily turn against us'. The Bengal Army differed from those of Bombay and Madras –

which gave no trouble in 1857 – in its large complement of upper-caste Hindus, whose sensibilities had been overridden by a regulation making future recruits liable for service overseas – e.g. in Burma, a routing which had twice been resisted for caste reasons. In a climate of change the fear of caste-breaking could be widened to a suspicion of Christianizing intentions, which in some cases pious British officers did nothing to dispel. Revolt among the sepoys was finally precipitated by rumours that the cartridges (which had to be bitten before loading) for the new rifle introduced in 1857 were greased with the fat of cows (sacred to Hindus) or pigs (a pollution to Muslims). Early incidents in the Calcutta area were thought to have been settled, when in May the scene shifted to Upper India and the Bengal Army's main recruiting-ground in disaffected Oudh. The outbreak at Meerut was mishandled, allowing the rebel troopers to advance unpursued to Delhi. At Cawnpore the British contingent was massacred under a flag of truce, but at Lucknow Sir Henry Lawrence had provisioned the Residency for its historic siege. Daunting situations faced the scattered British over a wide area of Northern India, but in the Punjab John Lawrence and his officers dramatically disarmed 36,000 restive sepoys, fully replacing them by Sikhs – whose support for their recent conquerors was a decisive factor – and by tribal irregulars.

150 Huge lions guard the Roorkee aqueduct near the head of the Ganges Canal, projected and constructed by Sir P. T. Cautley and opened for four hundred miles in 1854. Today it irrigates two million acres and provides hydroelectric power, while Cautley's Roorkee training college has become an engineering university.

151, 152 Sepoys of the Company's forces (right) engaged on the British side during the revolt of 1857–8. British and Indian troops jointly achieved the storming of Delhi (below), where the mutineers in occupation outnumbered them by three to one.

A symbolic focus of revolt was found in Delhi, where the last scion of the House of Timur, the aged Bahadur Shah II, lingered querulously as a pensioner of the British. The rebel seizure of the city was made easy – and its recapture correspondingly arduous – by the siting of the British military and civil station outside (but the magazine inside) the walls, which had been strengthened by British engineers. The proclamation of Bahadur Shah as emperor helped to swell the rebel garrison with continuous reinforcements from the south and east. The siege and eventual storming of the city from the north was a signal feat of arms, and its sacking a signal act of savagery – in both of which the Government's British and Indian troops shared almost equally. Together with the recovery of Cawnpore (one day too late to prevent the slaughter of captive British women and children), and the first relief of Lucknow at the end of September, this meant that the back of the Mutiny had been broken in four months, and before the arrival of seaborne rein forcements. The British had survived a terrible summer, but there was much bitter fighting to come. The final recapture of Lucknow was achieved in March 1858, the campaign in Central India lasted until June, and guerilla resistance continued in several districts till the end of that year.

153 Lucknow, chief city of Oudh, in ruins after its recapture by the British in March 1858. The Residency had been relieved in the previous September after withstanding a bitter siege.

154 Queen Victoria in 1873, seated on an ivory throne presented to her by the Maharaja of Travancore.

THE VICTORIAN ZENITH

The upsurge in Northern India had drawn upon different elements of discontent, but the view that it was a national revolt can hardly survive the fact that it failed. The British were never entirely alone, and while the rebels had fighting spirit their counsels were divided and their leadership local or non-existent. The darkest and the brightest pages on their side of the account were recorded by the dispossessed – the darkest at Cawnpore by the Nana Saheb, whose pension as the deposed Maratha Peshwa's adopted heir had been discontinued: the brightest in Central India by the Rani of Jhansi, who died at the head of her last cavalry charge to earn praise from her British opponents and a romantic fame among her countrymen. The part played by the last Moghul, who was tried for it and exiled to Rangoon, was scarcely his own. Nearly all the Princes, faced with the question of what might follow the extinction of the foreign power, opted for the *status quo*: and the *status quo* was in fact their reward. An assurance that there would be no more encroachments on their lands and rights was given in the proclamation of Queen Victoria which in 1858 marked the

transfer of authority from the now anomalous Company to the Crown. Prestige was mutually enhanced in 1876, when the Queen was declared empress of India. In 1911 her grandson George V received as king-emperor the homage of the Princes in a great durbar at Delhi: to which historic site, he then announced, the capital of the Indian Empire would be transferred from metropolitan Calcutta.

In Canning's view of the Mutiny the Princes were 'break-waters in the storm'; and it was politic to preserve them as such. This freezing of history, for which the governor-general assumed the additional title and functions of viceroy as the personal link in a feudal relationship, gave the Victorian empire its unique glitter and its constitutional complexity. If it continued the vices of the subsidiary system in granting Indian rulers security without responsibility, it also gave scope, in an 'Indian India' occupying 38·5 per cent of the total territory, for the traditional virtues of personal rule, and for cultural continuity against the Westernizing tide. As a conservative reassurance, however, it symbolized the damage done by insurrection to the ideas of progress based on English education and the example of British institutions:

155 Lord Canning, governor-general and first viceroy, visiting the Maharaja of Kashmir, Hindu ruler of a largely Muslim population, in 1866.

145

the process that was to lead, in Macaulay's famous phrase, to 'the proudest day in English history' when India should outgrow the rule of her political mentors.

Macaulay's prophetic occasion had been provided by the Charter Act of 1833, which established the eligibility of Indians for any appointment in the administration, but had no effect on the Company's practice of nomination. The substitution in 1853 of open competition began the refashioning of the Indian Civil Service, but the journey to England to study and take the examination was an obstacle to most Indian aspirants: so that although Victoria's 1858 Proclamation re-affirmed the principle, the first Indian was not admitted to the ICS until 1861, to be followed by three more in 1864. The system of appointment was eased in the 1880s. But above the subordinate level and the technical services of the railways, engineering, public works, forests, etc., the trickle of Indian entry only became a stream after World War I. Yet the middle classes had lent no support to the Mutiny, and their small but growing Westernized elite believed openly in the British Raj as a beneficent force for India's destiny. They continued to do so in face of the post-Mutiny tendency of British policy to desert the class it had created. The 'unofficial' Indian members who from 1861 were nominated to the central and provincial legislative councils in a consultative role, and to the organs of local self-government on which a start was made in 1873, were drawn to a large extent from the princely and land-holding classes. The very ability of the men produced by the system of English education came to be held against them, and the Bengali honorific of *babu* to be used in contempt. Lord Curzon, who began in 1899 a viceregal term distinguished by a drive for bureaucratic efficiency, confessed none the less that it was the 'cleverness' of this intellectual élite that he feared.

By that time the unofficial members of the legislative councils were less restricted in their function, and the elective principle had been in operation in urban and rural local government since the reforms of the Liberal Lord Ripon in 1883. It was Ripon, however, who had felt the crude force of a 'white backlash' to a measure (the so-called Ilbert Bill) for meeting the advance of Indians to the post of district judge with a consequential provision enabling them to try Europeans on criminal charges. The European mercantile community, and the tea-planters for whom restrictions on 'waste land' ownership had now been removed, had been increased by new arrivals with a post-Mutiny prejudice, and together they raised such a storm of threat and protest that the Viceroy stooped to a compromise. It was the worst public explosion, as distinct from private behaviour, of a racialism stemming from the events of 1857–8, when the Calcutta press had given the first of the viceroys the name – and not in praise – of 'Clemency' Canning. The ferocity of reaction at that time, Canning had reported, appeared to be in direct proportion to the distance from danger. In the unaffected centres of Madras and Bombay, however, relations had long been noted as more relaxed than in Calcutta; and Bombay in particular, now expanding into prosperity with the largely Indian-capitalized

cotton industry, had the valuable social leaven of the Parsi community. In a broader sense several factors – the opening of the Suez Canal in 1869, the development of hill-stations and the increase of Western amenities – brought more European wives and families into the picture and promoted a separate existence. If the higher services seemed aloof, they also kept a certain distance from their commercial compatriots, whose assault upon the Ilbert Bill nevertheless found support from Calcutta officials. But the ICS had also what its historian (Philip Woodruff) calls 'an ardent minority . . . who hated arrogance in any form and who believed that justice was not always done as between English and Indian.' Some of them spoke out boldly during their service. Others, like William Wedderburn, Henry Cotton, David Yule and Allan Octavian Hume, devoted their energetic retirement to an alliance with the English-educated leaders of Indian opinion. And it was Hume (who had retired to Simla instead of going 'home') who played the decisive part in the foundation in 1885 of the Indian National Congress, which he nursed through its infancy while insisting that its directive force should be Indian. This was the body, welcomed at its formation by the Viceroy (Lord Dufferin) that was to become the main instrument of the movement for independence, and the party of majority government after its achievement.

A clear consequence of the Mutiny was seen in military reorganization. The proportion of Indian to British troops at the outbreak had been more than five to one. They were now equalized in the Bengal Army, and in Madras and Bombay set as one European unit to two Indian ones (British-officered). The former Company's European

156 First meeting of the Indian National Congress, in Bombay, December 1885. 'The founders of the Congress', wrote an Indian historian, R.P. Masani, 'were proud to describe it as an offspring of British rule.'

troops, having expressed their objections to the terms of Crown service by a 'white mutiny', took their discharge, and the new pattern was maintained by brigading battalions from British regiments with their Indian counterparts. The Gurkha rifle regiments, recruited by treaty with Nepal, were included in the Indian Army, which from 1895 was unified by dissolving the old Presidency forces in regional commands. Despite such initial evidence of mistrust as the retention of the artillery in British hands, the new army was welded into the proud and reliable force that served on several fronts in two world wars, and in the Second was expanded without conscription from 200,000 to nearly $2\frac{1}{2}$ million men. From 1932 it had its own military academy at Dehra Dun, and the delayed 'Indianization' of King's Commissions went rapidly ahead, with results that were important for the two new dominions fifteen years later. Except for the abortive formation by Subhas Chandra Bose, in 1943, of an Indian National Army from among prisoners humiliated by the surrender of Singapore to the Japanese, the Indian Army stayed clear of political involvement and contributed to mutual respect between the races. Its chief invitations to nationalist criticism were its professional exclusiveness and its high cost.

Most of that cost was incurred in the defence of the north-western frontiers, or in such probings beyond them as the Second Afghan War of 1878–80, in search of a settlement of respective spheres of influence and a 'scientific' frontier along which the steady advance of Russian power could be held. The wasteful strategic controversies of two decades were eventually settled politically, by the diplomatic recognition by both Britain and Russia of a buffer state of Afghanistan with defined frontiers, leading to the Anglo-Russian Convention of 1907. India's north-west frontier, however, was not an ethnic one; its tribal characteristics were strongly various, and the successful control of the Sind-Baluchistan border could not be repeated among the Pathans and other professional marauders on both flanks of the Khyber, who could draw arms and encouragement through Afghanistan. The frontier legend familiarized by Kipling continued as a lethal game of tangled codes and shifting tactics, combining 'Danegeld' with military and eventually air operations: a running drain on lives and resources and a major determinant in respect of training, organization and strategic communications.

The annexation of Upper Burma after the Third Burmese War of 1885 was the British answer to French expansion in Indo-China and intrigues at the Burmese court, but no serious threat to India in the north-east was conceivable before the Japanese operations of World War II. The formidable natural obstacle of the central Himalayas was unnecessarily overcome by the Younghusband Expedition to Lhasa in 1904 (before the Anglo-Russian Convention). Intended by the forceful Viceroy Lord Curzon – in face of London's disapproval – to forestall Russian interference in Tibet, this adventure secured a British-Indian presence in that hitherto closed country while allowing the dying Manchu Empire to assert for a few years its vague claims to suzerainty.

157 Opposite, above: the Bala Hisar fort at Kabul, photographed from the British Residency during the Second Afghan War, which accomplished nothing except the defeat of the 'forward school' of British policy in India towards the Russian advance in Central Asia.

158 Opposite, below: the trans-Himalayan expedition to Tibet in 1904, the last attempt to forestall an apprehended Russian approach to the Indian frontiers.

The Indian National Congress was twenty years old when, in 1905, it first admitted the constitutional future as a subject of discussion. Under the rising pressure of an extremist wing it then emerged from its advocacy of isolated reforms (with the avowed object of consolidating the union with Britain) to adopt the aim of self-government within the empire. This was the effective beginning of political nationalism, and also – with the foundation of the All-India Muslim League in 1906 – of the problem that was to dog the enterprise to the end of the road.

The flashpoint was found in the 1905 partition of Bengal, one of the last acts of Lord Curzon, a viceroy whose sincere but outdated imperialism had an ambiguous impact which still intrigues historians. His exaltation of the idea of India, his readiness to contest policies initiated in London, his quixotic defence of legal justice between the races and his signal contribution to national self-esteem by the rescue and preservation of the monuments of past glory, all helped to stimulate the mood of renascence: which, at the same time, he repeatedly offended by his unconcealed belief in British superiority, as a matter not simply of power and experience but of moral character. The division of a large and populous province was accepted by some officials as what the nationalist opposition believed it to be – an attack on the movement in its Bengal heartland. To Curzon it was a sensible administrative operation, conducted in bland indifference to Indian feelings. He was surprised at the reaction that it provoked, indignant when it led, a few years after his resignation, to abrogation of the partition. He did not live to witness the historic irony of 1947, when the dividing line was drawn again, this time as a state boundary, by agreement between the Congress and the Muslim League.

In 1905 the protests had a markedly Hindu ring which helped to range the Muslims of Bengal on the side of authority. 'Mother India' was a Bengali discovery of the Hindu revival. The songs and slogans and patriotic literature had a Hindu inspiration. The cult of the great Bengali mystic Ramakrishna exerted a nation-building influence of a new kind, and had been interpreted by his English-speaking disciple Vivekananda, on missions to Europe and America, with an effect that began the association of Hindu spiritual tradition with India's claim to a modern identity. (The curious hybrid of Theosophy, with similar premises, was presently to provide Mrs Annie Besant with an Indian political platform on the Home Rule ticket.) In reality the communal atmosphere in Bengal before the partition was less divisive than in Upper India, where Swami Dayanand's Arya Samaj, which had taken root in the Punjab in the 1870s, had a certain anti-Muslim content, reinforced in the next decade by a proliferation of explicitly communal cow-protection societies. Speaking broadly, however, the Muslim quarter of India's population was fifty years behind the Hindus in the growth of a modernizing professional and commercial middle class, and the injection of a political factor inevitably fostered fears that any British concession of democratic institutions would lead to domination by the Hindu majority. In a bid to make up the leeway Syed

159 Lord Curzon, energetic epitome of the imperial spirit; viceroy from 1899 to 1904, reappointed in December 1904, he resigned in October 1905.

Ahmad Khan had founded in 1875, with the help of the Nizam, the Mohammedan Anglo-Oriental College at Aligarh, and this became the first centre for the defensive tactics which reduced, though they could never wholly extinguish, Muslim participation in the Congress. At the same period a general expansion of education, on Indian initiatives and with official grants-in-aid, was producing a lower middle class with access to Western ideas but with little chance of employ-ment and still less of reaching the affluence represented by the moderate Congress leadership. This furnished a popular following for the extremist faction fostered in western India by B. G. Tilak, who deli-berately chose a communal basis for political activities, with the Maratha Shivaji as cult-hero and the Hindu god Ganesha as patron.

It was Tilak who anticipated the Gandhian logic of the alien Govern-ment's vulnerability to a widespread withdrawal of public co-opera-tion; and it was he who carried to Bengal, with a reputation enhanced by a prison term for sedition, the serviceable weapon of boycott. The anti-partition demonstrations were crushed with a severity which in its turn was to bring out the young terrorists of bomb and pistol, dedicated to Shiva or to Kali and fired by the philosophic eloquence of Auro-bindo Ghosh. But in Britain the Liberal landslide of 1906 brought signs of an intention to respond in some way to Congress aspirations. The germ of an elective principle had already been secreted in the otherwise cautious Indian Councils Act of 1892, and the new Muslim League now sought, and received, assurances of separate electorates for Muslims and a 'weightage' to compensate their minority. On the face of it the device was undemocratic and anti-national, and its incorporation in the Morley–Minto Reforms of 1908–9 – named for the Liberal Secretary of State and the Conservative Viceroy – has often been seen as the cause, rather than the consequence, of triangular deadlock. Yet it was not opposed by the Congress, hopefully led by the moderate G. K. Gokhale and more concerned to subdue its own extremists; and in 1916, when Gokhale's death had left the field free to Tilak, a Congress–League pact conceded the idea of separate electorates in the bid for active unity. Tilak died in 1920, and it was left to Gandhi, emerging at the age of fifty with a new style of leadership, to seize what he saw as a golden chance for communal harmony by enlisting Con-gress support for the *Khilafat* agitation – the rallying of Indian Muslims on behalf of the Islamic caliphate of the Sultan of Turkey, threatened with extinction by the Allied peace terms. It was a deeply felt issue, but a bizarre attachment to the experiment in 'non-violent non-co-operation' with which Gandhi set out to confront the British Raj in India with the spirit of passive resistance which he had successfully kindled in South Africa before the First World War. In the end it was the Turks themselves who abolished the caliphate; while in India communal tensions increased in the aftermath of an anti-Govern-ment operation which Gandhi had called off on the idealistic ground that it had led to violence.

This was the first of three major and evenly spaced campaigns (1920–21, 1930, 1942) which supplied India's advance to indepen-

160 Mahatma Gandhi under a spinning-wheel flag at Ahmad-abad during the first civil dis-obedience campaign, 1921.

dence with the psychologically important element of struggle. Though apparently in stark conflict with the constitutional development – and so regarded, or rhetorically disregarded, by British authority – the phases of upsurge were in effect complementary to the process marked by the Montagu–Chelmsford Reforms of 1919, the elaborate federal project of 1935 and the Draft Declaration (the Cripps Offer) of 1942. Bounded by two world wars, the transition drew its first impetus from India's contribution to the preservation of the empire, which produced such acknowledgments of national identity as the nomination of Indian delegates to Lloyd George's War Cabinet, the Imperial Conference, the Peace Conference and the League of Nations. In August 1917 the British Government's policy was announced to Parliament as 'the gradual development of self-governing institutions with a view to the progressive realization of responsible government in India as an integral part of the British Empire'. Towards this radical, though guarded, advance the 1919 Reforms increased the representative and elective character of the central and provincial legislatures, and in the latter, by the innovation known as 'dyarchy', transferred all but certain reserved departments to Indian ministers. But the atmosphere had been profoundly changed by World War I, the end of the Russian, Austrian, German and Ottoman empires, American participation and the principle of national self-determination invoked for Europe; while India had to suffer the introduction of contentious security laws and the tragic shock of counter-violence in the Punjab disturbances of April 1919. Higher condemnation of General Dyer's action in firing upon an unarmed crowd at Amritsar, and of other extremities of repression, came too slowly to appease the sense of outrage which Gandhi was able to harness to his non-co-operation campaign. He had already changed the Congress structure from an élite political club into a mass organization, in which his influence rested on a power of popular appeal that was demonstrably unique.

By its boycott of elections under the reformed Constitution – the first act of a withdrawal aimed finally to paralyse government – this new Congress Party left the councils to be filled by more moderate elements and condemned itself to relative sterility when direct action was exhausted and the dynamic Gandhi was politically off-scene, whether in custody or in devotion to communal peace, the plight of the untouchables, and rural regeneration by the spinning-wheel. The issue so ardently argued after 1929 – Purna Swaraj (full independence) as against the 'natural objective' of Dominion status which Lord Irwin, as viceroy, extracted from the Labour Cabinet in London – was for Gandhi something of an irrelevance. But under the rising star of Jawaharlal Nehru the initiative in a divided Congress had passed to the younger left. Gandhi therefore resurfaced, abandoning compromise in order to control the upsurge, and launched the 1930 civil disobedience with his famous Salt March. Defying the fiscal laws by gathering salt from the sea, he initiated a largely non-violent but serious struggle which diverted world attention from the less dramatic Round Table Conference. This had assembled in London delegates from

161, 162 Opposite: the humiliations of repression in the Punjab (above), even more than the Amritsar massacre of April 1919 which they followed, provided the background against which Gandhi secured leadership for himself and his methods in the nationalist movement. The Salt March on which he set out from Ahmadabad with a picked body of followers (below) drew world-wide attention to the second wave of protest in 1930.

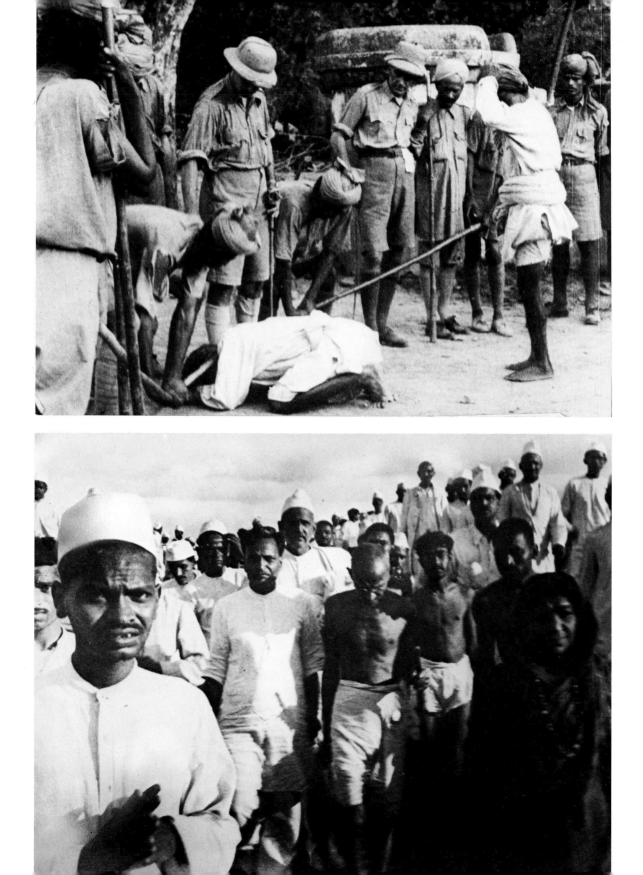

163 The Round Table Conference on the Indian Constitution in session in London in 1931. Gandhi, sole delegate from the Congress, sits at the chairman's left.

every Indian interest except the recalcitrant party that claimed to voice the national will; and Congress participation was one of the Viceroy's objectives when he eventually released its imprisoned leaders and invited Gandhi to New Delhi for the face-to-face talks which were long remembered as a gleam of sincerity, goodwill and trust. In the end, however, Gandhi went alone to the second Round Table session in 1931, and his impact was slight.

From a later standpoint an Indian historian (K. M. Panikkar) could write that by 1935, when the Act providing for a federal constitution reached the statute-book, 'British authority in India was in full retreat, in the administrative field no less than in the political and economic fields.' The Act itself was a landmark, and its value was to be proved when India came to frame its own independent constitution. But although the Congress brought itself in 1936–7 to take advantage of its most substantial provision – the conversion of the provincial adminis-trations to full autonomy on the parliamentary system – it remained hostile to the Act as a whole, and suspicious of British intentions until almost the brink of freedom.

The theory that Indian divisiveness in general, and the Muslim problem in particular, were creations of the ruling power for its own perpetuation, was understandable in the circumstances. But the Congress's consequent failure to take the Muslim question seriously while conciliation was still feasible approached a fateful point with the return as president of the Muslim League of the gifted Bombay lawyer M. A. Jinnah, who had been hailed as 'ambassador of Hindu-Muslim unity' before he withdrew in disillusion from the politics of the 1920s. He now took a weak League into the new elections on a temperate programme aimed at a share of democratic power, but fared poorly against rivals for the Muslim vote. The massive Congress appeal to both general and special electorates enabled them to form governments in seven of the eleven provinces, a height from which they saw no reason to meet Jinnah's expectation of coalitions. In making dissociation from the League a condition of office for Muslims, the Congress brought its principled status as the party of All-India nationalism into final confrontation with the League's claim to speak for the Muslims. Thenceforward Jinnah applied himself to convert Muslim apprehensions of Hindu majority rule, which was now equated with the Congress position, into a coherent and popular movement under his own control. The idea of Pakistan had already been academically conceived, but it was not adopted as League policy until 1940, and even then remained ill-defined. By August 1947 Pakistan was in being, in the Muslim majority zones of the north-west and the east. A threatened culture, labelled a minority, had been renamed a nation and vested with a state, itself divided. At midnight on 14-15 August 1947, a few hours after the installation of Qaid-i-Azam Jinnah as governor-general of the Dominion of Pakistan, the Congress pledge of Indian independence was redeemed, in Nehru's words, 'not in full measure but very substantially', and the last viceroy of the British Indian Empire accepted at his hands the invitation to serve the new Dominion as its first governor-general. In the months that followed some ten million people were on the move in both directions across the partitioned Punjab (see p. 159).

No such vivisection had been in the script for that measured devolution of imperial authority which in 1939 had been interrupted by war. From that point the mind and nerve of Jinnah had been concentrated on the denial of constitutional power to his opponents, and the Congress in effect abetted him by denying it to themselves. The withdrawal of the Congress provincial ministries was a principled response to inadequate political assurances as a condition for co-operation in the war, but the Thanksgiving Day promptly proclaimed by Jinnah showed where the advantage would thereafter lie. The two British efforts to bridge the gap at critical junctures – Linlithgow's 'August Offer' of 1940 and the Cripps Mission early in 1942, after the fall of Singapore – offered the first slight opening to secession from a post-war, Indian-made constitution. Both failed, and in the trough after each the Congress found its only escape from inaction in civil disobedience, conducted with restraint in 1940 but as 'open rebellion' in 1942, when the 'Quit India' campaign took a violent turn after the removal by arrest of Gandhi and the whole leadership. Though Gandhi was

164 Muhammad Ali Jinnah, Congress member until 1920, leader of the Muslim League from 1934, architect of a separate Pakistan and its first governor-general in 1947.

165 Police in Calcutta using tear-gas to disperse rioters attacking a Hindu temple during the murderous communal outbreak of August 1946.

released by Lord Wavell, Linlithgow's successor, in May 1944, the largest Indian party remained an illegal organization, and its politicians behind bars, until the Allied victory in Europe a year later allowed political talks to be resumed.

Fortunately for India's immediate survival, the dispute did not affect recruitment or war supplies, though for a time the vital north-eastern defence was endangered by severed communications. In the long run it could doubtless be said that the Congress, while losing ground to the pressure for Pakistan, preserved its ideological prestige as the party of Indian liberation: not only as against the Indian Communists, who were tied by Moscow directives to support of the existing Government for the Allied war-effort, but also as against the rival revolutionary appeal of direct action in collaboration with the Japanese. But in 1945 its leaders carried into the arena of complex negotiation a load of isolation and mistrust which, matched by the immobility of Jinnah, defeated first the efforts of Wavell, and next year those of a Cabinet mission sent by the Attlee Labour Government that in Britain had succeeded the Churchill War Coalition. Though the Viceroy managed to form an interim Government of Congress and Muslim League ministers, it proved unworkable, and in the face of murderous rioting (the 'Great Calcutta Killing' of August 1946) Wavell advised London to force a decision by fixing a date for complete British with-drawal. Attlee took his advice but replaced him by a new viceroy, Lord Mountbatten, giving him the plenipotentiary powers on which he insisted. In the meantime the wave of communal ferocity moved up the Ganges plain, spreading the infection for the first time among the rural populations, giving the aged Mahatma his 'finest hour' of lonely

166 Dr Rajendra Prasad (left), who was to be elected as the first president of the Republic of India, with Pandit Jawaharlal Nehru at a meeting of the Constituent Assembly, 1946/7.

conciliation in one area after another, and at length convincing Nehru and Vallabhai Patel, the key figures in the Congress, that some form of Pakistan would be preferable to anarchy. It is against that menacing background that the advance of the date for transferring power to August 1947, and the controversial speed of the immense operation, have to be judged. Significant among Mountbatten's personal achieve‑ ments was his persuasion of nearly all the Princes, whose procrasti‑ nation had prevented the completion of the 1935 Federation, that the paramountcy in which they trusted must lapse with the British de‑ parture. Had the Maharaja of Kashmir accepted the advice to accede before 15 August to either Pakistan or India (the Nizam of Hyderabad, the other large state, also postponed decision) the gravest obstacle to future peace would almost certainly have been avoided.

The transformed atmosphere of the British transfer of power to the Indian Constituent Assembly, and the popular rejoicing that almost overwhelmed the stately proceedings in New Delhi, revealed to the world at large something of a relationship unique in history between the former rulers and the former ruled: a shared experience which Dr Rajendra Prasad, soon to be the first president of the Indian Republic, placed in context in replying to the message of the last king‑emperor, George VI:

While our achievement is in no small measure due to our sufferings and sacrifices, it is also the result of world forces and events; and last, but not least, it is the consummation and fulfilment of the historic traditions and democratic ideals of the British race.

CHAPTER NINE

The new India

FREEDOM BY DIVISION

The devolution of power which in August 1947 brought into being the independent Dominion of India, concurrently with that of Pakistan, was a key event of history. By a separate process Ceylon (now Sri Lanka) became a Dominion early in the following year, while Burma, liberated from the Japanese by British and Indian forces, accepted the option of independence outside the Commonwealth. At the meeting of Commonwealth Prime Ministers in London in 1948 a formula was agreed for retaining India's membership after its adoption (1950) of the constitution of a federal republic, and the precedent thus established was followed in course of time by Pakistan and other new states. A pattern had been set for the transformation by consent of the multiracial British world-empire.

The effect of speed and resolution in laying this foundation, before the post-war consolidation of ideological power-blocs, can be judged by the contrasting path of Indo-China's emergence from European control. The price of the operation in the Indian subcontinent had nevertheless to be paid in bloodshed and suffering in the divided Punjab. Failure by the three main parties in the settlement to give due weight to the aspirations of the Sikhs provided a starting-point for the desperate migration of populations, which neither of the new Govern-ments desired, and which a joint force of fifty thousand troops was unable to control. In the aftermath of the transfer of power some five million Hindus and Sikhs moved eastwards out of Pakistan, and a similarly huge number of Muslims fled westwards from India, with a mutual infliction of atrocities costing a probable half-million lives. Delhi itself might have been overwhelmed by communal violence but for the presence, from October 1947, of Mahatma Gandhi. His work of pacification had shown results when, in January 1948, his great life was ended by a young Hindu extremist, incensed by the Mahatma's protection of the Muslim community. Much had been owed to Gandhi, also, in the relative tranquillity of the Bengal partition that created East Pakistan, though here too nearly half a million Hindus migrated from their homes.

The force of psychological shock on which Gandhi had often counted was seen for the last time in a general recession of the tide of violence from the impact of his assassination. But the problems of divi-

167 Opposite: Mrs Indira Gan-dhi, only daughter of independent India's first prime minister, Nehru, became prime minister herself in 1966. She is seen at the Delhi celebrations of the twenty-fifth anniversary of independence in 1972, addressing the crowd from the summit of Shah Jahan's Red Fort, with the Friday Mosque in the distance.

sion were by no means over. The resettlement of refugees was an added burden to both Governments as they faced the economic consequences of a partition which disrupted the pattern of communications and of production, separating (for example) India's mills from Pakistan's jute and cotton. The movement of peoples in the north, without eliminating the communal obstacle (forty million Muslims remained in the new India and eight million Hindus in Pakistan) left raw grievances on both sides. Such vital issues as regional defence, which demanded trust between the two states, produced for lack of it a doubly damaging load of expenditure and a mutually hostile distortion of policies. One important source of friction, concerning the distribution of canal, waters in the divided Punjab, was ended in 1961 with World Bank help. But the problem of Kashmir defied solution or mediation, from the point in October 1947 when its hesitant Maharaja appealed to India to intervene against a tribal invasion launched with the apparent connivance of Pakistan. The state's accession to the Indian Union – a requisite for rescue – brought regular Pakistan forces to confront the troops flown in from India; and the most that the United Nations could promote was a cease-fire on a line which left the western and north-western regions under Pakistan's *de facto* control, and to India the larger remainder, including Buddhist Ladakh in the north-east and in the centre – the main bone of contention – the famous and fertile Vale of Kashmir.

As Prime Minister of the Indian Union (with which he combined overall direction of foreign policy) Jawaharlal Nehru maintained a rigid attitude on Kashmir. To admit the religious factor of the state's Muslim majority as invalidating its legal accession to India would place the secular basis of the Indian Union in doubt and its non-Hindu subjects in peril. In other words, the pragmatic partition that created the two wings of Pakistan was the tolerable limit for the dreaded 'Balkanization' of the former British-Indian Empire. Consolidation of the remainder dictated the remarkably effective transactions, with Sardar Vallabhai Patel taking the chief responsibility, in which 562 princely states were incorporated in various forms in the federal Union, with compensation for their former rulers – as also the integration by 'police action' of Hyderabad, whose Nizam had held out for special status. Negotiation secured the eventual transfer to Indian authority of the small French enclaves of Pondicherry and Chandernagar, but in respect of Goa Portugal declined to recognize the end of the era initiated by Vasco da Gama. After six years of adherence to the principle of seeking a peaceful settlement, Nehru in December 1961 yielded to internal pressure, and defied external criticism, by annexing Goa with a show of force. A more intractable problem was posed in the north-east, where the British had left the tribal areas largely unadministered, and the Nagas and some other frontier peoples generated active resistance to any encroachment on their independence. A Nagaland state was brought into the Union under Nehru, and other groups were incorporated after his death, but not without tarnishing the Central Government's image by military severity and political censorship. The

168 Opposite, above: the end of the British Raj. Lord and Lady Mountbatten mobbed by happy crowds in New Delhi on Independence Day, 15 August 1947.

169 Opposite, below: 'The light has gone out of our lives.' Prayers beside the body of Mahatma Gandhi, assassinated in the garden of Birla House, New Delhi, on 30 January 1948.

location of this sensitive area between East Pakistan and a frontier disputed by the Chinese power added an obvious element of tension.

Alerted by divided independence to the dangers of further fission, the
assembly that evolved India's impressively elaborate Constitution
provided a strong federal centre: a departure not simply from the Gandhian vision of 'village democracy' but from such previous proposals
as those of the British Cabinet Mission in 1946, when the pacification
of Muslim separatism was still an object. At the same time the new Constitution pronounced upon fundamental aims and freedoms, and against
any discrimination on grounds of caste or religion. The way was thus
opened for tackling, within a large programme of social legislation,
the sort of reform from which the alien rulers (with exceptions which
have been noted) had been deterred by scruples against interference.
The historically unifying function of the caste system, which might have
commended itself at this juncture, was overshadowed for the Congress
modernizers, and above all for Nehru, by its hard core of patently
divisive force which Gandhi had combated with the faith and courage
of an outstanding Hindu reformer. The untouchables and other
'depressed classes' could not be redeemed by merely illegalizing their
plight. But Gandhi had stirred the national conscience on their behalf,
and although this and other forms of the system's grip continued to be
felt and seen, its loosening – abetted also by economic change – was
now only a matter of time. Dramatic changes in the status of women also
owed much to Gandhi, who had drawn so many from seclusion to
participate in struggle and social work. The first ministers and state
governors already included women of political experience; but Nehru
had to fight entrenched opposition through several sessions to break the
hold of the Hindu code by legislation on property rights, divorce and
widows' remarriage.

The most insidious threat to a secure adjustment of 'unity in diversity'
proved to be linguistic, and in two forms. The first arose from the inheritance of English as the vehicle of government and higher education,
a *lingua franca* for the upper and middle classes, the cement of unity
in the national revival, and a passport for India's entry into a modern
world community. The process had not depressed the regional languages,
which had benefited from the extension of printing and the great
proliferation of newpapers, and were now specifically encouraged in
their literary aspect. But there was no single and practicable indigenous
alternative to English in the national sense. The nearest was the generic
Hindi which broadly allied the chief spoken languages of Northern
India (tending after the partition to detach itself from the Persianized
Urdu), and the Constitution envisaged its replacement of English as
the official language by 1965 or earlier. Nehru (who died in 1964) was
concerned not only with the international, technological and scientific
value of English, but with the risks that would be run in forcing Hindi
upon the peoples of the South, tenaciously attached to the several forms
of their Dravidian heritage, and to English as the only acceptable
second language. His persuasive authority prevented a premature
cleavage, but violent rioting in the South answered the pro-Hindi

170 Sardar Vallabhai Patel, right-wing Congress leader, home minister and states minister, who was responsible for the integration of the princely states in the Indian Union.

utterances of his less tactful successor, Lal Bahadur Shastri. The turmoil subsided, but the problem remained.

Its other form had meanwhile been reflected in the redistribution of the states of the Union. The basic operation, under Patel as states minister, had formed out of nine former provinces and the newly integrated princely states a pattern of twenty-seven states of the Union. By 1953, however, various clamours for revision led to public consultation by a States Reorganization Commission which uncovered, not without misgiving, a passionate demand for the linguistic principle of statehood, complicated by the competition for economic assets (the city of Bombay, for example, was finally included in Maharashtra against the contention of Gujarat). From 1956 the Indian Union thus came to consist of fourteen states, later increased to sixteen, with nine smaller centrally administered territories. Further changes after Nehru's death included a late surrender to Sikh agitation for the linguistic division of India's portion of the Punjab.

THE SHAPE OF DEVELOPMENT

It was a combination of stability, flexibility and progressive impulse which carried independent India, with setbacks but without catastrophe, through its first quarter-century. Survival in a dangerous world confirmed, by and large, the revolutionary validity of what Marxists had from the first denigrated as 'national-bourgeois reformism'. Though this would not have happened without the evolution under British rule of a Westernizing middle class, the avoidance of the postulated 'second revolution' depended largely upon the link which Gandhi had established with the rural masses, and to some extent with the relatively small urban proletariat. It was Gandhi, in these terms, who had decided that national and social revolution were inseparable. Neither his final dissociation from the Congress as a party of power, nor the disparities between his decentralized, non-violent utopia and the India of Five-Year Plans and sixty-per-cent defence budgets, prevented the bequest of popular leadership in the person of Nehru, and of a nation-wide Congress organization that proved too valuable an asset to be allowed to lapse.

Successive general elections, conducted in an exemplary manner on the gigantic scale of an unrestricted adult franchise, confirmed a commanding Congress majority in the central and state legislatures. The Communists, for whom (after the failure of 'direct action') Moscow policy sanctioned the pursuit of the 'constitutional path', provided the official opposition at the centre (and from 1957 to 1959 enjoyed electoral majority in the southern state of Kerala).

The factor of Nehru's leadership, the magic of his name and the energy of his character, had clearly been all-important. Without counting his interim office in the preface to independence, he was at the head of his country's affairs for seventeen years – for the first three in a so-called 'duumvirate' with the right-wing Congress veteran Patel, whose death in 1950 left Nehru's constitutional and popular ascendancy unchallenged. In contrast Pakistan had to suffer the death of Jinnah and the assassination of his ablest statesman, Liaqat Ali Khan, within four years of independence.

To Nehru the meaningful revolution for the consummation of India's 'tryst with destiny' was the technological one. In his outgrowth of early Marxist influences there were several elements: his temperamental (and Cambridge-educated) humanism and distaste for doctrinaire solutions; his emotional bond with Gandhi that transcended differences; and his rejection, as a dedicated nationalist, of the external direction for which he berated the Indian Communists while developing a liberal internationalism. But the Soviet example of planned development, on a subcontinental scale and involving multi-ethnic and depressed populations, stayed with him; and the ambition to achieve no less by democratic means – without forced savings, forced labour and the sacrifice of intellectual and social liberties – derived added urgency from the competition of Communist China. For the survival outside the Western world of the ideals of an open society, the Indian enterprise was crucial.

India had the considerable initial advantage of having been spared the devastations of war, though the indirect disaster of the 1943 Bengal famine had been sufficiently appalling. With eighty per cent of the population compressed in a static and debt-loaded agricultural system, the task of producing a dynamic economy on the modern pattern was formidable. But the industrial base and infrastructure existed, internal capitalization had been advancing for some time, and the war-time stimulation of production had done something to remedy the ill balance of a semi-dependent economy. Important raw materials were abundant, human resources incalculable in their potential, administrative and managerial experience awaiting only the opportunity of expansion.

171 Symbols allotted to political parties and independent candidates enable the illiterate part of the population to vote. The Congress party symbol, two bulls with a yoke, is at the top left, with the Communist symbol below it.

172 A polling station.

173 Nehru inaugurating a Community Development Project, organized on Gandhian principles of rural self-help with official co-operation.

174 Above, right: a slum clearance enterprise in South India.

175 Opposite: manpower at work on the Tungabhadra dam (Andhra and Mysore) with an irrigation potential of 1,030,000 acres, one of more than eighty major water and power projects undertaken in the first two decades of independence.

Though Nehru eventually moved to the proposition of a 'socialist pattern of society', the government and party which he led was too broad in its association of all but the extremes of right and left to be saddled with a socialist *policy*. The principles of a mixed economy were established at the outset, in the division of the field of development into state, private and joint sectors. The main emphasis of the First Five-Year Plan, launched in 1951, was on agriculture, with targets set for irrigation, fertilizers and road-building. The irrigation schemes of the British period had been the largest in the world, yet no more than six per cent of the flow of India's great rivers had been harnessed, and there were the losses from partition to be made good. The First Plan brought an additional seven million acres under irrigation, with multi-purpose projects greatly expanding generating capacity. The rise of eighteen per cent in the national income over these five years was reckoned as twice the increase in population. The switch of pressure to industry in the much larger Second Plan (which was to include three new million-ton-capacity steelworks, respectively assisted by Britain, West Germany and the USSR) was therefore made in some confidence that the worst problems of food-supply had been overcome.

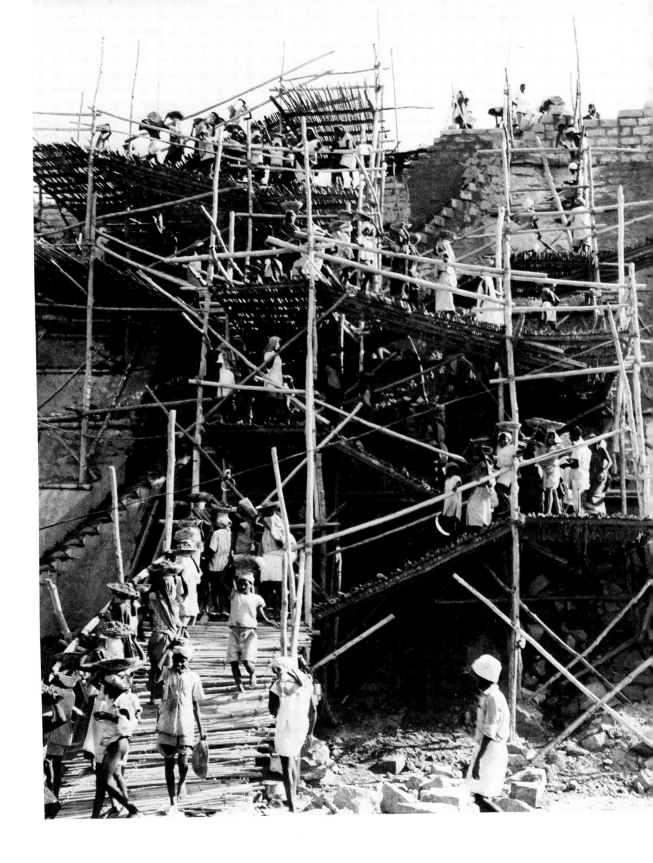

176 Man and industry. A scene at Durgapur, one of the three great state-owned steel plants built since the late 1950s with British, West German and Soviet assistance.

This was a miscalculation. Although some economists hold that the main industrial drive should have had greater priority, the solution of age-old agrarian ills in a climate of persuasion was not within the compass of centralized planning. Much was indeed accomplished, in a variable combination of bureaucracy with the Gandhian heritage of local initiative. But India's eternal dependence on the monsoon rains provided another form of statistical defiance. Severe drought in 1955–6 extended foodgrain rationing to 230 million people and brought famine conditions to Bihar; and demographic error – by postponing a concerted attack upon the fundamental population issue – contributed to the difficulties over the decade (1961–71) of the Third and Fourth Plans. The death-rate, which had been almost halved by medical advance and health measures in the last twenty-five years of British rule, was almost halved again by their expansion in the first twenty-five years of independence. With the birth-rate declining far more slowly – indeed it showed a slight increase in the 1950s – the pressure on land and resources threatened every victory gained in the fight against poverty.

The broader effects of education – a major field of expansion for which the states retained constitutional responsibility – were not easy to assess. Beyond the obvious target of literacy (where the figure was doubled to thirty per cent of the population over the first quarter-century of independence) Nehru's belief in the political education of an illiterate majority by the exercise of the vote was at least partly justified. The provision in various forms of free primary schooling throughout the country paid tribute to a plan elaborated by the last British Secretary for Education. But the effects of top-heaviness and the dominating arts-degree tradition, which had shown themselves in the former system, did not vanish with the multiplication of India's universities to a total of seventy. Technical colleges and scientific research institutes, however, were an important feature of the drive for modernization, and it was Nehru's personal interest that gave impetus to the development of atomic energy at Bombay. The moral principles that confined this outstanding enterprise to peaceful purposes were to come under question with the entry of the Chinese into the field of nuclear weaponry. But India's idealism was backed by calculation, and it held.

177 Nursery school in Chandigarh, the new capital built for India's part of the Punjab after Lahore had gone to Pakistan.

India's requirements of foreign exchange, and of foreign aid, trade and co-operation in various forms, were a natural (though unexpressed) factor in the international policy for which the Nehru administration provided the foundations and guidelines. Three-quarters of the resources for funding the development plans were found internally, with a strategic use of deficit budgeting and high upper-income taxation. In financial terms India had been turned by war purchases into a substantial creditor of the United Kingdom, and drawings on these sterling balances were the largest single source of foreign exchange during the first two Plans. The exodus of British officials was far more than replaced by the increasing influx of British businessmen and technicians, operating under new 'risk' conditions which guaranteed high-grade employment and majority shareholdings for Indians but produced a British investment of roughly twice what it had been before independence, representing nearly eighty per cent of all private foreign capital in the country. The Colombo Plan for Economic and Technical

178 The highway to Katmandu, a link between Nepal and India constructed under the Colombo Plan.

Co-operation in South-East Asia was a pioneering approach, under Commonwealth auspices, to regional development on a basis of equality and reciprocity. Canada, and to a lesser degree Australia and New Zealand, were early contributors of credit and assistance for Indian development. But this was only one aspect of the potential of a free Commonwealth – the 'silken bond' which Gandhi had extolled and which Nehru and his colleagues accepted as a valuable extension of India's position, offering a range of advantages with no political constraint. Apart from the United Nations, where India found a prominent role both politically and in the specialized agencies, the Commonwealth offered the one form of association that could tolerate India's choice of a non-aligned 'abstention from power-blocs' and preserve it from becoming a position of withdrawal. The evidence of a continuing trend in the devolution of British imperial power proved sufficient to sustain India's support of the Commonwealth, though there were obstacles to smooth relations in the essentially impartial attitude of the United Kingdom towards Indo-Pakistani differences. And the policy as propounded by Nehru survived periodical strains (with the Suez crisis of 1956 as an acute example) to be bequeathed to his immediate successors as a tested principle.

The stance of non-alignment, which in the context of 'free world' resistance to Communist expansion was treated in both camps as a heresy, did not prevent large and indeed vital contributions to India's growth and sustenance from the United States – most of it either in straight grants or 'soft' loans and supplemented by releases from American food surpluses. The Soviet view of the Nehru Government as a 'camp-follower of imperialism' was modified after the death of Stalin, and from 1955 Soviet credits (confined to the 'public sector') made their mark upon India's development, on a far smaller scale than Western co-operation but with persuasively low interest-rates. In political terms, and with changes in the international power pattern, the assumptions of non-alignment came at length to be recognized by the outside world as relevant to India's situation, and indeed as having contributed to the avoidance of nuclear war.

The doctrine of 'Peaceful Co-Existence' was enunciated at the 1955 Conference of Asian Governments (and a few African representatives) at Bandung in Indonesia, in the aftermath of the Korea and Indo-China wars. While the stand against outside interference taken by the emergent Asian states at Bandung produced a measure of accommodation in the policy of Communist China, the part played by Nehru and his delegation revealed to Peking a potential rival for leadership in Asia. India had already indicated, by renewing relationships with the Himalayan states of Nepal, Sikkim and Bhutan, its acceptance of the British imperial bequest. But the trans-Himalayan extension of the Raj's influence to Tibet had been less defensible in Nehru's eyes, so that a compromise with Peking's 'sovereignty' or 'suzerainty' (the words provided barren argument) was regarded as a reasonable price for the objective of good relations between the two largest nations. Except on the most superficial level, however, Sino-Indian understanding was

179 Indian soldiers patrolling the cease-fire line in remote Ladakh. The rivalry of Mao's China, breaking into frontier war in 1962, enormously increased India's defence problems and expense.

never achieved. Amicable frontier adjustments were excluded by the menacing uncertainties of a Chinese approach that called the entire frontier into question as a relic of the rejected past, challenging India's relationships with the Himalayan states, and opening to question the large eastern sector of loosely administered tribal territory. Tibet provided the crux of the matter by its strategic and political importance to the Chinese Government, and by the sympathies inevitably engaged in India by the gradual revelation of Tibetan resistance to the destruction of their uniquely religious society. While Nehru's 'appeasement' of the Chinese had thus to face internal criticism, the crisis of the Lhasa revolt in 1959, and the escape of the Dalai Lama to sanctuary in India, were treated by Peking as proof of Indian interference. In the climax of undeclared war in October–November 1962, a double Chinese offensive gained ground on the uninhabited heights of Ladakh, and in the eastern sector of the long mountain-frontier inflicted on India first military defeat and then – with China's unilateral cease-fire and withdrawal of her invading forces – political humiliation.

This unexpected manœuvre (though classic precedents could have been found in Chinese history) had some success in its purpose of weakening India at a time when the Chinese Communists were themselves facing isolation by the widening breach with Moscow. The last two years of Nehru's life, in the ruins of his China policy, were a painful struggle with old age and declining powers, from which the country would not allow him to seek refuge in retirement. The promptness

180 Nehru with the Soviet leader Marshal Bulganin in Moscow in 1955, a visit that was returned by Bulganin and Khrushchev. Indo-Soviet relations were further developed after the conflict with the Chinese People's Republic.

with which, at the point of India's peril, British military assistance had been offered and accepted as if by an unspoken Commonwealth right, seemed also to undermine a central principle of 'non-alignment'. Encouragement could be drawn from the staunchness of popular response in the crisis. But although the Communist Party of India found itself once more compromised by divided loyalties (and was itself to be divided by the widening Peking-Moscow rift), India's constitutional freedoms had been dented by the introduction of emergency restraints. It was of great significance, on the other hand, that the Indian Army's record of abstention from politics survived the strains which elsewhere produced the familiar pattern of 'colonels' revolts'.

While the need for a tolerable accord with China had been exhibited, its attainment had been indefinitely postponed. The same could be said of India's relations with Pakistan, whose adherence to US-sponsored defence pacts for West and South-East Asia – suspected in Delhi as an anti-Indian device – were ignored in the ideologically bizarre association now developing between Pakistan and China. The importance of India's strategic communications with Ladakh, through the great wedge of disputed Kashmir, had been emphasized, and the reorganization and strengthening of frontier defences was undertaken in an exacerbated version of the same political context – simultaneous confrontation with both Pakistan and China – that had bedevilled the past.

CHAPTER TEN

India after Nehru

THE DYNASTIC SUCCESSION

It was Nehru's successor – the little-known Lal Bahadur Shastri – who in August–September 1965 had to meet the trial of armed strength with Pakistan which the changed situation had presaged. After an unsteady beginning in foreign affairs, he displayed some diplomatic finesse by mending fences with Nepal, consolidating India's standing in the Non-Aligned Movement that Nehru had founded along with Yugoslavia and Egypt, and making a successful visit to London. He showed great firmness in the war that raged briefly across ancient battlefields in the divided Punjab. Both air forces were engaged, and there were naval skirmishes. But India made no move against Pakistan's vulnerable eastern wing, consisting of East Bengal and the Sylhet district – an immunity Pakistanis attributed to the inactive but threatening proximity of their new Chinese allies. Since neither India nor Pakistan could face a prolonged war without replacement of their foreign-made military hardware and spare parts, withheld by the manufacturing nations, the fighting on both sides was fierce and expensive, but short. A ceasefire achieved under UN auspices was followed by a successful meeting in January 1966 of both sides in Tashkent, capital of the Soviet Republic of Uzbekistan, with the Soviet leader Leonid Brezhnev presiding. This signalled the emergence of the Soviet Union as the sponsor of an Asian settlement, an unprecedented event. Shastri's sudden death in the Uzbek capital then brought into power Nehru's daughter, Mrs Indira Priyadarshani Gandhi, who defeated her rival Morarji Desai decisively, thanks to the older power-brokers of the Congress who thought that, lacking a proper political base of her own, she would do their bidding.

Once in power, Mrs Gandhi surprised her colleagues and adversaries by her ability to manoeuvre and manipulate. Those skills of hers, however, failed to save the Congress from the drubbing that it received in the 1967 general election. Its strength shrank from 317 to 281 in a Parliament of 480 MPs. It lost power to anti-Congress coalitions in nine major states containing two-thirds of the national population. In 1969 the Congress split, with the right-wingers — led by Desai and calling for an alliance with rightist opposition groups and the bolstering of the private sector – defecting and turning Indira Gandhi's Congress into a minority party in the central Parliament. Mrs Gandhi survived with the support of forty-three Communist MPs belonging to the pro-Moscow Communist Party of India and the independent-minded Communist Party of India (Marxist), who backed her decision to nationalize the top fourteen banks

181 Opposite: crowds fill New Delhi's vast processional way, laid out by the British, for the funeral of Jawaharlal Nehru in 1964. In the distance are the government buildings.

and to terminate the privileges and pensions that had been granted to the Princes in compensation for the surrender of their powers in 1947, which required amending the Constitution. With both Communist parties wedded to pursuing the parliamentary path to attain power, extra-parliamentary Communists organized themselves under the banner of the Communist Party of India (Marxist-Leninist), commonly known as Naxalites.

Riding a wave of popularity engendered partly by the easy lending terms that the newly nationalized banks offered to their customers of modest means, Mrs Gandhi called a mid-term poll in early 1971 and won nearly two-thirds of the seats in Parliament on the catchy slogan of 'Garibi Hatao' (Remove Poverty). About then, in Pakistan's eastern wing – more populous than its western counterpart – the long-smouldering Bengali demand for a more equitable status became a struggle for independence when the Pakistani military government tried to reverse the verdict of free elections by using force. During seven dreadful months Mrs Gandhi restrained her hand against the backdrop of internal clamour for intervention, while the unending flood of refugees from East Pakistan crossing into Indian protection rose to a staggering ten million. By the time she finally ordered the army to march into East Pakistan in December 1971, she had secured the almost unanimous support of Indian politicians. Swift success on both Pakistani fronts – east and west – and India's decision not to use the war for territorial gains, won further approval at home and abroad. Out of East Pakistan emerged Bangladesh (Country of Bengalis), with its sovereignty recognized internationally, except by Pakistan and China, and accepted as the newest member of the British Commonwealth (from which Pakistan withdrew) and as a friendly neighbour of India. Mrs Gandhi's reputation stood high. But the economic cost of the East Pakistani refugee crisis and the 1971 war with Pakistan had been heavy. On top of that came three years of drought and an annual inflation rate of thirty per cent, caused in part by a big jump in the oil price. The poorest among the populace suffered most. Prime Minister Gandhi tried to divert public attention by ordering the explosion of a nuclear device in the Rajasthan desert for 'peaceful purposes', with its fuel most probably processed from the waste products of the five-year-old Canadian-built nuclear power station at Tarapur, Maharashtra. The ploy failed, and the anti-government agitation gained momentum.

In June 1975 the High Court in Allahabad upheld the charges of electoral malpractices against Indira Gandhi in the 1971 parliamentary poll. This automatically barred her from office. After her lawyers had obtained a three-week postponement of the court order to allow Congress MPs to elect another leader, she had President Fakhruddin Ali Ahmed declare a national State of Emergency, thereby suspending the constitutional articles which guarantee protection of life and liberty. In a pre-dawn swoop, her Government arrested hundreds of opposition leaders and imposed strict censorship. Claiming that 'forces of disintegration' were rife, Mrs Gandhi declared curbing inflation, invigorating the economy and toning up civil administration as the aims of the Emergency.

182 Opposite: nuclear energy installations at Trombay, near Bombay. 'Power for every village in India' was Nehru's directive in 1961, and by 1974 reactor plants in three centres supplemented the hydro-electric expansion. Under Mrs Gandhi a nuclear device was exploded (with peaceful intentions stressed), and India's technological progress was seen in the launch of a communications satellite.

The poster content (as photographed): MARCH OF THE REPUBLIC · 1977 · Sovereign Democratic Republic · Sovereign Socialist Secular Democratic Republic · equal opportunity for all · equitable benefit from national resources to all · equal respect for all religions · OUR NEXT GOAL ECONOMIC FREEDOM

183 Indira Gandhi's Congress Party poster for the 1977 general election portrays her as the political heir and natural successor to her father, Nehru. Despite this emotive appeal, she was heavily defeated by the Janata Party (and lost her own seat in parliament).

By early 1976 the number of people imprisoned without trial had passed 125,000, twice the figure reached during the anti-British 'Quit India' agitation in 1942. Released from the accountability of a democratic system, the police took to arbitrary arrests and became more corrupt than before. Under the slogan of 'urban beautification', poor people were forcibly expelled from cities, and a programme of compulsory vasectomies was implemented under the leadership of twenty-seven-year-old Sanjay Gandhi, son of the prime minister. Due to the lack of a free press, police and intelligence services became the chief source of news-gathering for Indira Gandhi and her coterie. Based on their favourable reports on the Government's performance, and on an improvement in the economy caused by good harvests and an inflation rate of three per cent, Mrs Gandhi ordered the nation's sixth general election and ended the Emergency in January 1977.

The Congress faced the Janata Party, an amalgam of five major opposition groups, and lost heavily, winning not a single seat in northern India – where the sterilization programme had been forcefully implemented during the Emergency – including Indira Gandhi's constituency

YOUTH LEADER Sh. SANJAY GANDHI'S

FIVE POINTS PROGRAMME
★PLAN YOUR FAMILY ★MARRIAGE WITHOUT DOWRY
★ONE MAN, ONE TREE ★ EACH ONE TEACH ONE
★CAMPAIGN AGAINST CASTE SYSTEM
TALK LESS WORK MORE

DISTRICT YOUTH CONGRESS ARNAL

in Uttar Pradesh. The next prime minister was Morarji Desai. However, having ousted their common enemy, Indira Gandhi, from power, the constituents of the Janata Party began to bicker, and the Government fell. In the 1980 general election, Indira Gandhi was returned to power, having adroitly exploited the divisions within the Janata Party, which collapsed as a national organization. She was aided by her elder son Rajiv, an airline pilot, the younger, ambitious Sanjay having died while performing aerial stunts in a private plane over Delhi.

India's traditional paradoxes were again to be seen as Nehru's wish for a strong centre for the Union of Indian states transmuted into 'dynastic democracy', in which weak state governments felt hamstrung in their attempts to tackle the twin problems of bureaucratic inertia and a corrupt civil service. The linguistic reorganization of the states in 1956 had created homogeneous administrative units sharing the same culture – with a few exceptions, such as racially diverse Assam and bilingual Bombay and the Punjab. Within a decade, however, yielding to popular agitation, the Central Government agreed to divide these bilingual states respectively into Gujarat and Maharashtra, and into Punjabi-speaking

184 Sanjay Gandhi's Youth Congress election poster in Karnal, Haryana, sets out his political programme. The issue of compulsory vasectomies was a major contributor to the defeat of the Congress Party in the 1977 election.

185 In June 1983, a year before the storming of the Golden Temple in Amritsar, there were serious disturbances in the city. Here, a Sikh rioter is arrested by police, among whom are other Sikhs.

Punjab and Hindi-speaking Haryana. In the neighbouring independent island of Sri Lanka, communal passions were aroused between the minority Hindu Tamils and the majority Buddhist Sinhalese, a development which would later impact on Indian politics.

Despite the change of ruling parties in Delhi, India's non-aligned foreign policy remained unaltered. Membership of the British Commonwealth went hand in hand with stable relations with the West in general, but with a wariness towards America, which, however, continued to be the chief provider of food aid to India, supplying an average of six million tons of foodgrains, and with US President Richard Nixon writing off two-thirds of the $3.2 billion owed by Delhi in 1973. At the same time, India's relations with the Soviet Union remained strong, with the two countries signing a Friendship and Cooperation Treaty in August 1971, four months before Delhi's military intervention in East Pakistan, and Moscow becoming the largest supplier of weapons to

India. The launching of an Indian unmanned satellite with US-supplied components by a Soviet-supplied launcher rocket from the Baikonur Space Centre in Soviet Kazakhstan in 1975 neatly summed up Delhi's non-aligned foreign policy. In 1983, as the host of the triennial conference of the 76-member Non-Aligned Movement in Delhi, Indira Gandhi became the NAM president for the next three years. But she did not live to serve her full term. In October 1984 she was assassinated by two of her Sikh bodyguards in revenge for sending troops into the Golden Temple in Amritsar, the holiest shrine of Sikhs, to remove, in the midst of much bloodletting, armed Sikh militants who were committed to establishing an independent state of Khalistan (Land of Khalsa [Pure] Sikhs). A massacre of Sikhs ensued in Delhi and its suburbs and left 10,000–20,000 dead. Indira Gandhi's son Rajiv, now a junior MP, was sworn in as prime minister by President Zail Singh, a Sikh, and was then elected leader of the governing Congress Party in Parliament, an undemocratic procedure, symptomatic of the Nehru–Gandhi dynastic rule. Under Rajiv Gandhi, the Congress won the 1984 parliamentary poll on the sympathy vote.

186 Beant Singh, one of the Sikh bodyguards who assassinated Mrs Gandhi in October 1984, standing beside the prime minister during the official visit to India by the French President Valéry Giscard d'Estaing in January 1980.

Possessing neither the political cunning of his mother nor the intellect or vision of his maternal grandfather, Nehru, Rajiv Gandhi proved unequal to the position to which he had been catapulted. Soon his image as Mr Clean was soiled by a scandal concerning India's purchase of Swedish-made Bofors self-propelled artillery guns amidst allegations of kickbacks from the Bofors company to him and his cronies. Responding to a request for help from Sri Lanka, which was facing an armed insurgency by its Tamil minority, Rajiv Gandhi dispatched Indian troops to the island ostensibly for peace-keeping – a step condemned by the separatist Liberation Tigers of Tamil Elam.

In the uproar of the Bofors affair, Rajiv Gandhi's Congress lost the ninth general election in 1989 to the National Front, an alliance of several parties whose leader, Vishwanath Pratap Singh, became prime minister. But when he acted to implement an earlier recommendation on the reservation of civil service jobs for lower Hindu castes, he lost the backing of middle- and upper-caste Hindu MPs, and gave way to another National Front leader, Chandra Shekhar. He ruled briefly.

INTO THE TWENTY-FIRST CENTURY

In May 1991, during the run-up to the tenth general election, Rajiv Gandhi was assassinated in Madras (now Chenai) by a woman Tamil Tiger suicide bomber as retribution for the Indian troops' anti-Tamil intervention in Sri Lanka. The Congress Party, now led by Pamulaparti Venkata Narsimha Rao, won the general election, and Narsimha Rao became the first Indian prime minister from the South. Under him, economic liberalization, initiated by Rajiv Gandhi, gathered pace. He also normalized relations with China, thus removing the last remnants of tension between the two Asian giants.

In late 1992, against the background of rising Hindu nationalism in the country, nearly a quarter-million militant followers of the Vishva Hindu Parishad (World Hindu Council) stormed police barricades and

187 Militant Hindus stand triumphantly on the domes of the Babri Mosque in Ayodhya in December 1992. The subsequent demolition of the mosque led to serious conflict between Hindus and Muslims, threatening the secular basis of the republic.

tore apart the Babri Mosque, named after Emperor Babur, in Ayodhya, with a view to constructing a temple to Lord Rama, a native of Ayodhya by tradition, at the site. This was the worst challenge faced by secular India, made all the more potent by the anti-Muslim pogrom in Bombay (Mumbai) in January 1993 that claimed three thousand lives.

In the 1996 parliamentary poll, the Hindu nationalist Bharatiya Janata (Indian People's) Party, BJP, emerged as the largest single group in Parliament. Yet the next cabinet was formed by the larger United Front – an alliance of regional parties hastily cobbled together – led by H. D. Deve Gowda, another southern politician, who was soon followed by I. K. Gujral.

When the BJP again emerged as the single largest group in Parliament following the 1998 general election, it gathered thirteen other smaller groups under the umbrella of the National Democratic Alliance (NDA), which formed the Government led by Atal Behari Vajpayee. He ordered the detonation of an atomic bomb, thus making India the seventh nuclear nation – after America, Russia, Britain, France, China and Israel. Pakistan followed suit. Thus the Indian subcontinent came to acquire two nuclear powers. As required by its law, the United States imposed certain economic sanctions against both India and Pakistan for acquiring nuclear weapons.

When a few NDA constituents proved unruly, Vajpayee sought a fresh mandate in 1999. The NDA returned with a comfortable majority, with Vajpayee at the helm. The next year India faced renewed fighting –

first by proxy and then directly – with Pakistan in the northern Kargil region of Indian-administered Kashmir. It raised the prospect of an all-out war between the two nuclear-armed neighbours. US President Bill Clinton intervened, and this persuaded Pakistani Prime Minister Nawaz Sharif to withdraw his forces from Kargil.

Delhi accused Islamabad of training and infiltrating Kashmiri and non-Kashmiri fighters into Indian-administered Kashmir (with a population of nine million) – a process that began following the Soviet military withdrawal from Afghanistan in 1989, which the Afghan and non-Afghan Islamic fundamentalist fighters considered a victory for their *jihad* (holy war) against the Soviet Union. Islamabad denied the charge, arguing that Kashmiri militants were merely fighting for their right to self-determination, and that all they got from Pakistan was moral support. During the twelve years of Muslim separatist insurgency and governmental counter-insurgency, an estimated 30,000–40,000 people had been killed in Kashmir, where Delhi had deployed some 400,000 military and security personnel.

When, following the suicide attacks in September 2001 on the World Trade Center in New York and the Pentagon in Washington, US President George W. Bush launched a worldwide campaign against terrorism, India joined the coalition immediately, arguing that the source of terrorism committed in Kashmir and America was the same: a network of training camps in Afghanistan maintained by Osama bin Laden and his al-Qaeda organization.

Delhi thus rejuvenated the warm bond that Washington under President Clinton had forged with India in the aftermath of the collapse of the Soviet Union in late 1991, with a belated realization that, as a multi-party, secular democracy for nearly half a century, the Indian republic was a natural political ally of the United States. This revised perception of India, which had been diplomatically sidelined by Washington during the 1946–91 Cold War as a friend of Moscow, coincided with the information technology revolution that transformed American society, and to which India contributed by exporting to the US tens of thousands of its computer engineers graduating from Indian institutes of technology that had been established by Nehru soon after India became independent.

Since then, the life-expectancy of Indians has more than doubled, from thirty-two to sixty-eight years, and the literacy rate has risen to sixty-six per cent from a base of eighteen per cent. The country has made impressive gains in economic development and investment, achieving an average annual real economic growth rate of six per cent in the 1990s, partly due to economic liberalization initiated in the late 1980s. Today, it produces a wide array of industrial goods and military hardware, including ground-to-ground missiles and unmanned satellites. India became self-sufficient in food in the mid-1980s – two decades after the introduction of the Green Revolution, involving the planting of High Yield Variety (HYV) seeds of wheat and rice, with HYV seeds covering a third of the total wheat-growing area within five years, and raising the average yield nearly two-and-a-half times.

Yet, according to the 2001 census, more than a quarter of India's 1,071 million inhabitants live below the poverty line – as defined by the Government – and cannot afford an adequate diet. Nearly four-fifths of Indians continue to live in villages which often lack basic amenities such as running water; and seventy per cent of them depend on agriculture, which contributes only twenty-five per cent of the gross domestic product. Although the vigorously pursued, but voluntary, family-planning programme has reduced annual population growth to 1.6 per cent, the current density of 337 persons per square kilometre (130 per square mile) remains too high for an underdeveloped economy. Relations between the Hindu majority (seventy-eight per cent) and the Muslim minority (thirteen per cent) are far from harmonious, with tensions between the two communities periodically escalating into violence – as happened in Gujarat in 2002.

Socially, caste-consciousness remains strong among rural Hindus, who form the bulk of the population, with the age-old system of segregation whereby castes are housed intact in villages while outcastes and Muslims continue to be confined to separate hamlets away from the village. On the positive side, where caste is concerned, political power has seeped down from the upper brahman and kshatriya castes to middle and lower castes, reflecting a growing awareness among electors of the power of the vote, and among politicians of the importance of accountability.

Over the past five decades or more, democracy has struck roots in the Indian soil. Except for the 1975–77 Emergency, multi-faith, multi-lingual and multi-ethnic India has functioned as a political democracy in which the executive, legislative and judicial organs of the state remain separate, and where freedoms of speech, association and assembly are guaranteed by the constitution. Unlike in Pakistan, the military in India has remained aloof from politics, with the generals accepting civilian leadership without question. Independent India has discarded the British idea of 'martial races' in recruitment to the military, which remains a voluntary force. Even if Indian politicians wanted it, the country cannot afford the compulsory military training imparted to all adults as is the case in China, which is already an economic giant.

The Washington-led war launched in October 2001 against the regime of the Taliban of Afghanistan – an extremist Islamic fundamentalist movement harbouring Osama bin Laden, accused of masterminding terrorist attacks on the US – brought Pakistan into focus, partly because of the long Afghan–Pakistan border, and partly because the Taliban had been created and sustained by Islamabad. Fearing disastrous consequences if America declared Pakistan a nation supporting international terrorism, its military ruler General Pervez Musharraf sided with the US and severed links with the Taliban. Two months into the American air campaign, Kashmiri terrorists attacked the Indian Parliament. Delhi accused two Pakistan-based organizations – Lashkar-e Taiba (Army of the Pious) and Jaish-e Muhammad (Army of the Prophet Muhammad), committed to securing Kashmir's secession from India – of responsibility for the outrage, and demanded immediate action by Musharraf. When he prevaricated, India threatened war and mobil-

ized its army. Pakistan reciprocated. Washington intervened. Musharraf banned these organizations, thus delinking the Kashmiri separatist insurgency from the pan-Islamist *jihad*. This improved the chance of a peaceful resolution of the Kashmir dispute – an undeclared prerequisite for India's permanent membership of the United Nations Security Council, a long-held aspiration of Delhi.

As a member of the World Trade Organization, India is part of the globalization that is sweeping the economies of most nations and creating an international division of labour. In the emerging economic order, India is set to become a front-runner in the information technology and concomitant communications explosion as a result of the comparatively low cost of training and employing its scientists, engineers and technicians. Domestically, this is likely to expand the already wide gap between the haves and the have-nots, with the former increasingly opting for consumerism and Western values, and the latter, including a rising number of educated young people, often unemployed or underemployed, resenting their poverty. Whether India's socio-political system will be able to contain the rising tensions as the twenty-first century unfolds is an open question.

188 The information technology explosion has made India the second largest provider of software in the world. Here, in March 2000, a billboard offering a 'cool life' through computer training rises incongruously above a squatter settlement in Bangalore.

Select Bibliography

GENERAL WORKS

Cambridge History of India, ed. Haig *et al.*, 6 vol. (Cambridge, 1922–32);
    Shorter History, ed. Dodwell (Cambridge, 1934)
Chaudhuri, N. C. *The Continent of Circe* (London, 1965)
Davies, C. C. *An Historical Atlas of India* (Oxford, 1949)
De Bary, W. T. *et al. Sources of Indian Tradition* (New York, 1958)
Edwardes, M. *A History of India* (London, 1961)
Eliot, H. M. and Dowson, J. *History of India as told by its own Historians*,
    6 vol. (Cambridge, 1931)
Garratt, G. T. (ed.). *The Legacy of India* (Oxford, 1937)
Majumdar, R. C. (ed.). *The History and Culture of the Indian People*, 7 vol.
    (Bombay, 1957)
Nehru, J. *The Discovery of India* (London and New York, 1946)
Philips, C. H. *Historians of India, Pakistan and Ceylon* (London, 1961)
Powell-Price, J. C. *A History of India* (London, 1955)
Rawlinson, H. G. *India, a Short Cultural History* (London, 1952)
Singhal, D. P. *India and World Civilization*, 2 vol. (London, 1972)
Spate, O. H. K. *Geography of India and Pakistan* (London, 1957)
Thapar, R. (vol. 1) and Spear, P. (vol. 2). *A History of India* (Harmonds-
    worth, 1965–6)

SPECIAL AND REGIONAL STUDIES

Ambedkar, B. R. *The Untouchables* (Delhi, 1948)
Caroe, Sir O. K. *The Pathans* (London, 1958)
Chaitanya, K. *A New History of Sanskrit Literature* (Bombay, 1962)
Conze, E. *Buddhism* (Oxford, 1951)
Elwin, V. *India's N-E Frontier in the 19th Century* (Oxford, 1960); *The
    Tribal World of Verrier Elwin* (Oxford, 1964)
Herklots, G. A. *Islam in India* (new ed. Oxford, 1928)
Hunter, Sir W. W. *The Indian Musulmans* (new ed. London, 1945)
Hutton, J. H. *Caste in India* (Cambridge, 1946)
Misra, B. P. *The Indian Middle Classes* (London, 1961)
Majumdar, R. C. *History of Bengal* (Dacca, 1943)
Panikkar, K. M. *Asia and Western Dominance* (London, 1953)
Radhakrishnan, S. *The Hindu View of Life* (London, 1927)
Rowland, B. *The Art and Architecture of India* (Harmondsworth, 1968)
Salatore, B. A. *The Wild Tribes of Indian History* (Lahore, 1935)
Sardesai, G. S. *A New History of the Mahrattas*, 3 vol. (Bombay, 1946)
Sastri, K. A. N. *A History of South India* (Madras, 1955)

Sastry, K.R.R. *Indian States* (Allahabad, 1941)

Sen, S.P. *The French in India* (Calcutta, 1946)

Singh, K. *The Sikhs* (London, 1953)

Tandon, P. *Punjabi Century* (London, 1965)

Thomas, P. *Christians and Christianity in India and Pakistan* (London, 1954)

Tod, Sir J. *Annals and Antiquities of Rajasthan* (new ed. London, 1960)

Tuker, Sir F. *Gorkha* (London, 1958)

Zaehner, R.C. *Hinduism* (Oxford, 1962)

ANCIENT AND PRE-ISLAMIC INDIA

Basham, A.L. *The Wonder that was India* (London, 1954)

Coomaraswamy, A.K. *Buddha and the Gospel of Buddhism* (New York, 1916)

Cunningham, Sir A. *The Ancient Geography of India* (London, 1871)

Derrett, D. *The Hoysalas* (Oxford, 1957)

Dutt, N.K. *The Aryanisation of India* (Calcutta, 1925)

Dutt, S. *Buddhist Monks and Monasteries of India* (London, 1962)

Giles, K.A.(tr.). *The Travels of Fa-hsien* (Cambridge, 1923)

Keith, A.B. *Religion and Philosophy of the Veda and Upanishads* (Cambridge, Mass., 1925)

Kosambi, D.D. *The Culture and Civilisation of Ancient India in Historical Outline* (London, 1965)

Mackay, E. *Early Indus Civilisation* (London, 1948)

MacNicol, N. *Hindu Scriptures* (London, 1938)

Majumdar, A.K. *The Chalukyas of Gujarat* (Bombay, 1956)

Majumdar, R.C. *Ancient Indian Colonies in S-E Asia* (Baroda, 1955)

Majumdar, R.C. (ed.). *The Vedic Age* and *The Age of Imperial Unity* (Bombay, 1951)

Marshall, Sir J. *Mohenjo-daro and the Indus Civilisation* (London, 1931)

McCrindle, J.W. *Ancient India as Described in Classical Literature* (London, 1901)

Mookerjee, R.K. *Chandragupta Maurya and his Times* (Madras, 1943); *Harsha* (Oxford, 1925); *The Gupta Empire* (Bombay, 1947)

Narain, A.K. *The Indo-Greeks* (Oxford, 1957)

Piggott, S. *Prehistoric India* (London, 1950)

Rawlinson, H.G. *Intercourse between India and the Western World* (Cambridge, 1916)

Sastri, K.A.N. *The Cholas*, 2 vol. (2nd ed., Madras, 1955); *The Mauryas and Satavahanas* (London, 1959); *The Pandyan Kingdom* (London, 1929)

Schroff, W.H. (tr.). *The Periplus of the Erythrean Sea* (London, 1912)

Sen, A. *Asoka's Edicts* (Calcutta, 1956)

Shrava, H. *The Sakas in India* (Lahore, 1947)

Sinha, B.P. *The Decline of the Kingdom of Magadha* (Patna, 1954)

Smith, V.A. *Asoka* (3rd ed., Oxford, 1920)

Tarn, W.W. *Alexander the Great*, 2 vol. (Cambridge, 1948); *The Greeks in Bactria and India* (London, 1938)

Thapar, R. *Asoka and the Decline of the Mauryas* (Oxford, 1960)

Thomas, E.J. *The Life of Buddha as Legend and History* (New York, 1927)

Wales, H. G. Q. *The Making of Greater India* (London, 1931); *Towards Angkor* (London, 1937)

Wheeler, Sir R. E. M. *Civilization of the Indus Valley and Beyond* (London, 1966); *Early India and Pakistan* (London, 1959); *The Indus Civilization* (3rd ed., Cambridge, 1968)

Yazdani, G. (ed.). *The Early History of the Deccan* (London, 1960)

THE MOGHUL EMPIRE AND ITS PREDECESSORS

Aiyangar, S. K. *South India and her Muhammadan Invaders* (Madras, 1921)

Ahmad, M. A. *Political History and Institutions of the Early Turkish Empire of Delhi* (Lahore, 1949)

Babur (tr. Beveridge). *Memoirs* (London, 1921)

Bernier, F. *Travels in the Mogol Empire*, ed. Smith and Constable (Oxford, 1934)

Binyon, L. *Akbar* (London, 1932)

Duff, G. *History of the Marathas* (London, 1826)

Erskine, W. *Babur and Humayun*, 2 vol. (London, 1854)

Foster, Sir W. *Early Travels in India* (London, 1921); *The Embassy of Sir T. Roe to India* (London, 1926)

Habibullah, A. B. M. *The Foundations of Muslim Rule in India* (Lahore, 1949)

Husain, A. M. *The Rise and Fall of Muhammad bin Tughluq* (London, 1938)

Ikram, S. M. *Muslim Civilization in India* (New York, 1964)

Lane-Poole, S. *Medieval India under Mohammedan Rule* (New York, 1903)

Moreland, W. E. *From Akbar to Aurangzeb* (London, 1923); *India at the Death of Akbar* (London, 1920)

Prasad, Beni. *History of Jahangir* (London, 1922)

Qanungo, K. R. *Sher Shah* (Calcutta, 1921)

Qureshi, I. H. *The Administration of the Sultanate of Delhi* (Lahore, 1945)

Rawlinson, H. G. *British Beginnings in Western India* (Oxford, 1920); *Shivaji the Maratha* (Oxford, 1925)

Sarkar, Sir J. *History of Aurangzeb*, 5 vol. (Calcutta, 1952)

Sewell, R. *A Forgotten Empire* (London, 1900)

Smith, V. A. *Akbar the Great Mogul* (Oxford, 1927)

Williams, L. F. Rushbrook. *An Empire Builder of the Sixteenth Century* (London, 1918)

THE BRITISH PERIOD

Andrews, C. F. and Mukerji, A. *Rise and Growth of Congress in India* (Bombay, 1938)

Anstey, V. *The Economic Development of India* (3rd ed., London, 1949)

Aspinall, A. *Cornwallis in Bengal* (Oxford, 1918)

Bolitho, H. *Jinnah* (London, 1954)

Chaudhuri, N. C. *The Autobiography of an Unknown Indian* (London, 1951)

Coupland, R. *The Constitutional Problem in India* (Oxford, 1944)

Davies, A. M. *Clive of Plassey* (Oxford, 1939)

Davies, C. C. *Warren Hastings and Oudh* (Oxford, 1939); *The Problem of the North-West Frontier* (Oxford, 1932)

Dodwell, H. H. *Dupleix and Clive* (London, 1920); *The Nabobs of Madras* (London, 1926)

Dutt, R. C. *The Economic History of India in the Victorian Age* (London, 1906)

Edwardes, M. *The Last Years of British India* (London, 1963); *The Orchid House* (London, 1969)

Embree, A. *Charles Grant and British Rule in India* (New York, 1962)

Feiling, K. *Warren Hastings* (London, 1954)

Furber, H. *John Company at Work* (Cambridge, 1948)

Gandhi, M. K. *The Story of My Experiments with Truth* (London, 1949)

Gopal, S. *The Viceroyalty of Lord Irwin* (Oxford, 1957); *The Viceroyalty of Lord Ripon* (Oxford, 1953)

Griffiths, Sir P. J. *The British Impact on India* (London, 1952)

Ilbert, Sir C. *The Government of India* (London, 1916)

Kaye, J. W. *History of the War in Afghanistan*, 3 vol. (London, 1851)

Kaye, J. W. and Malleson, G. B. *History of the Indian Mutiny* (London, 1897)

Keene, H. G. *Hindustan Under the Freelances* (London, 1907)

Kripalani, K. R. *Tagore, Gandhi and Nehru* (Bombay, 1947)

Lambrick, H. T. *Sir C. Napier and Sind* (Oxford, 1952)

Malcolm, Sir J. *Memoir of Central India*, 2 vol. (London, 1828)

Masani, R. P. *Britain in India* (Oxford, 1960)

Mayhew, A. *The Education of India* (London, 1926)

Montagu, E. S. *An Indian Diary* (London, 1930)

Moon, Sir P. *Gandhi and Modern India* (London, 1968); *Warren Hastings and British India* (London, 1954)

Morrison, J. L. *Henry Lawrence* (London, 1934)

Nanda, B. R. *Mahatma Gandhi,* (London, 1958); *The Nehrus, Motilal and Jawaharlal* (London, 1962)

Nehru, J. *An Autobiography* (London, 1942)

O'Malley, L. S. S. *Modern India and the West* (London, 1941)

Pandey, B. N. *The Break-Up of British India* (London, 1969)

Philips, C. H. (ed.). *The Evolution of India and Pakistan* (London, 1962)

Polak, H. S. L. *et al. Mahatma Gandhi* (London, 1949)

Roberts, Lord. *Forty-One Years in India* (London, 1897)

Roberts, P. E. *A History of British India* (Oxford, 1932); *India under Wellesley* (Oxford, 1929)

Ronaldshay, Lord. *Life of Lord Curzon*, 2 vol. (London, 1928)

Sarkar, Sir J. *The Fall of the Mughal Empire* (Calcutta, 1950)

Sen, S. N. *The Indian Mutiny* (Delhi, 1957)

Singh, K. *Ranjit Singh* (London, 1962)

Smith, R. B. *Life of Lord Lawrence*, 2 vol. (London, 1885)

Spear, P. *The Nabobs* (rev. ed., Oxford, 1963); *Twilight of the Mughals* (Cambridge, 1951); *Oxford History of Modern India* (Oxford, 1964)

Tahmankar, D. V. *Lokamaniya Tilak* (London, 1956)

Thompson, E. *Life of Charles, Lord Metcalfe* (London, 1937); *The Making of the Indian Princes* (Oxford, 1943); *The Other Side of the Medal* (London, 1925)

Thompson, E. and Garratt, G. T. *The Rise and Fulfilment of British Rule in India* (London, 1934)

Tyson, G. *India Arms for Victory* (London, 1944)

Warner, Sir W. L. *Life of Lord Dalhousie* (London, 1904)

Watson, F. *The Trial of Mr Gandhi* (London, 1969)

Wavell, Lord (ed. Moon). *The Wavell Diaries* (London, 1973)
Wolpert, S. A. *Tilak and Gokhale* (Berkeley, 1962)
Woodruff, P. *The Men Who Ruled India*, 2 vol. (London, 1953–4)

TRANSFER AND INDEPENDENCE

Akbar, M. J. *Nehru: The Making of India* (London, 1988)
Bains, S. J. *India's International Disputes* (London, 1962)
Brass, P. *The Politics of India since Independence* (Cambridge, 1994)
Brecher, M. *Nehru, a Political Biography* (Oxford, 1959); *The Struggle for Kashmir* (New York, 1953)
Brown, J. M. *Modern India: The Origins of an Asian Democracy* (Oxford, 1985)
Campbell-Johnson, A. *Mission with Mountbatten* (London, 1951)
Ganguly, S. *The Crisis in Kashmir: Portents of War, Hopes of Peace* (Cambridge, 1999)
Gopal, R. *India-China-Tibet Triangle* (Lucknow, 1964)
Griffiths, Sir P. J. *Modern India* (2nd ed., London, 1965)
Hiro, D. *Inside India Today* (London, 1976); *The Untouchables of India* (London, 1982)
Iyengar, S. K. *Fifteen Years of Democratic Planning*, 2 vol. (London, 1966)
Jones, W. H. M. *Parliament in India* (London, 1957)
Joshi, G. N. *The Constitution of India* (3rd ed., London, 1954)
Jussawalla, A. (ed.) *New Writing in India* (Harmondsworth, 1974)
Keay, J. *India: A History* (London, 2000)
Khilnani, S. *The Idea of India* (London, 1997)
Korbel, J. *Danger in Kashmir* (Princeton, 1954)
Levi, W. *Free India in Asia* (Minneapolis, Minn., 1952)
Lumby, E. W. R. *The Transfer of Power in India* (London, 1954)
Mallick, R. *Indian Communism: Opposition, Collaboration and Institutionalization* (Delhi, 1995)
Masani, M. R. *The Communist Party of India* (London, 1954)
Mason, P. (ed.). *India and Ceylon: Unity and Diversity* (London, 1967)
Maxwell, N. *India's China War* (London, 1970)
Menon, V. P. *The Integration of the Indian States* (Calcutta, 1956); *The Transfer of Power in India* (Calcutta, 1957)
Moon, Sir P. *Divide and Quit* (London, 1961)
Mosley, L. *The Last Days of the British Raj* (London, 1962)
Panikkar, K. M. *The Foundations of New India* (London, 1963)
Read, A. and Fisher, D. *The Proudest Day: India's Long Road to Independence* (London, 1998)
Segal, R. *The Crisis of India* (London, 1967)
Spear, P. *A History of India*, Vol. 2 (Harmondsworth, 1970); *India, Pakistan and the West* (4th ed., Oxford, 1967)
Tinker, H. *India and Pakistan* (London, 1962)
Tuker, Sir F. *While Memory Serves* (London, 1950)
Tyson, G. *Nehru, the Years of Power* (London, 1966)
Ward, B. *India and the West* (London, 1961)
Wirsing, R. G. *India, Pakistan and the Kashmir Dispute* (Basingstoke and New York, 1994)
Wolpert, S. A. *A New History of India* (New York, 1982)
Zinkin, M. *Development for Free Asia* (London, 1963)
Zinkin, M. and T. *Britain and India* (London, 1964)

1 Map of the Indian peninsula. *Drawn by Hanni Bailey*

2 Lion-capital from a pillar erected by the Emperor Ashoka, 3rd century BC. Sarnath Museum. *Photo Martin Hürlimann from his book Asia (London, 1957)*

3 View of the Himalayas from the summit of Ratang Tower. *Photo J. Allan Cash*

4 Map of India showing the monsoon winds. *Drawn by Hanni Bailey, after C. Collin Davies, An Historical Atlas of the Indian Peninsula (Oxford University Press, 1949)*

5 Air view of the Ganges valley between Patna and Banaras. *Photo J. Allan Cash*

6 Approach of the monsoon over the river Kaveri, Deccan. *Photo Francis Watson*

7 Cardamom hills, South India. *Photo Victor Kennett*

8 Impression of a seal from Mohenjo-Daro showing a bull, 3rd millennium BC. British Museum, London

9 Bull of polished sandstone on the capital of a pillar erected by the Emperor Ashoka, from Rampurva, Bihar, 224 BC. National Museum, New Delhi

10 Stone statue of Nandi (16 feet high), on Chamundi hill, Mysore, 1659. *Photo Josephine Powell*

11 Gold coin from Jahangir's Zodiac series showing a bull, c. 1620. British Museum, London. *Photo Ray Gardner*

12 Bull and cow in a street in Calcutta. *Photo CTK/Camera Press*

13 *Colin Mackenzie with brahman assistants*, by Thomas Hickey. India Office Library, London

14 *James Prinsep surrounded by Hindu pundits*, by Sir Charles D'Oyley, 1823–9. India Office Library, London

15 Nagas at a village assembly meeting, Assam. *Photo R.J. Chinwalla/Camera Press*

16 Koli fisherman, Bombay. *Photo Bernard J. Silberstein/Camera Press*

17 Gond villager making fire. *Photo British Museum, London, Department of Ethnology*

18 A Toda village in the 1890s. India Office Library, London

19 Cromlechs at Rajan Kollur, Gulbarga District (Hyderabad); watercolour by Philip Meadows Taylor, 1850. India Office Library, London

20 Axonometric reconstruction of the great bath, Mohenjo-Daro, 3rd millennium BC. *Drawn by Peter Pratt*

21 Part of the drainage system at Mohenjo-Daro, 3rd millennium BC. *Photo Josephine Powell*

22 The citadel at Mohenjo-Daro, with the great bath in the foreground, 3rd millennium BC. *Photo Josephine Powell*

23 Map showing sites of the Indus valley culture. *Drawn by Hanni Bailey*

24 Seals from Mohenjo-Daro showing a 'unicorn', a rhinoceros, and a horned god, 3rd millennium BC. Museum of Pakistan, Karachi. *Photo Josephine Powell*

25 Jewellery from Harappa, 3rd millennium BC. The necklace is made of gold, semi-precious stones, and vitreous paste. National Museum, New Delhi

26 Painted vase from Harappa with a typical leaf pattern, 3rd millennium BC. *Photo Department of Archaeology, Agra, courtesy the India Office Library, London*

27 Bronze figurine of a dancing-girl from Mohenjo-Daro, 3rd–2nd millennium BC. National Museum, New Delhi

28 Steatite bust of a man from Mohenjo-Daro, 3rd millennium BC. National Museum of Pakistan, Karachi. *Photo Department of Archaeology, Government of India*

29 Goat of cast bronze from Mohenjo-Daro (left) and toy climbing monkey of carved terracotta from Harappa, with holes allowing it to move on a string, 3rd millennium BC. National Museum, New Delhi. *Photo courtesy the Royal Academy of Arts, London*

30 Sciopodas or one-legged monster, detail of woodcut from Sebastian Münster's *Cosmographia universalis*, 1544

31 Brahman priest reading the scriptures. *Photo Francis Watson*

32 Stone statue of Brahma from South India, 10th–11th century. The Metropolitan Museum of Art, New York, Eggleston Fund, 1927

33 Bronze statue of Shiva Vishapaharana, Chola, c. 950 AD. Shiva is warding off poison symbolized by the cobra on his left arm. British Museum, London

34 Bronze figurine of Ganesha from Madras, probably 10th century AD. Victoria and Albert Museum, London

35 Bronze figure of Hanuman from the Deccan, 11th–12th century AD. British Museum, London

36 A scene from the *Ramayana*, detail of a Hindu cotton temple-hanging from Mathura, c. 1800. Victoria and Albert Museum, London

37 King Parikshit and the rishis, an

episode from the tenth book of the *Bhagavata Purana*; southern Rajasthan (?), *c.* 1576. The Cleveland Museum of Art, Purchase, Mr and Mrs William H. Marlatt Fund

38 Buddha taming a mad elephant, railing medallion from Amaravati, 2nd century A D. Government Museum, Madras

39 Prince Siddhartha riding to school in a chariot, grey schist relief in Gandhara style, 2nd-4th century A D. Victoria and Albert Museum, London

40 Adoration of the Bodhi-tree, detail of a relief on one of the gateway pillars of the Great Stupa at Sanchi, 1st century A D. *Photo Martin Hürlimann*

41 Tibetan pilgrim at Bodh Gaya. *Photo Francis Watson*

42 Red sandstone relief showing homage to the *Dharmachakra*, from Mathura, 2nd century B C. Victoria and Albert Museum, London

43 Stupa at Sarnath, 6th century A D. *Photo Barbara Wace*

44 Mountain defile at Tashkurghan, Afghanistan

45 Alexander the Great, obverse of a silver tetradrachm of Lysimachus, king of Thrace, *c.* 290 B C. Bibliothèque Nationale, Paris. *Photo Archives Photographiques*

46 King Porus attacked by Alexander, obverse of a silver decadrachm of Alexander minted at Babylon, *c.* 326 B C. British Museum, London. *Photo Peter Clayton*

47 Terracotta figurine of a woman wearing an elaborate headdress and a dress with panniers, from Pataliputra, *c.* 200 B C. Patna Museum

48 Chariot-wheel excavated at Pataliputra, 3rd century B C. *Photo Archaeological Survey of India, courtesy the India Office Library, London*

49 Rock at Girnar carved with an Ashokan inscription, watercolour by Thomas Postans, 1838. India Office Library, London

50 Ashokan pillar at Lauriya Nandangarh, 243 B C. *Photo Archae-*

ological Survey of India, courtesy the India Office Library, London

51 Entrance to the Lomas Rishi cave in the Barabar hills, 3rd century B C. *Photo Archaeological Survey of India, courtesy the India Office Library, London*

52 Eastern gateway of the Great Stupa, Sanchi, 1st century B C. *Photo Hans Hinz, Basel*

53 Menander of Bactria, obverse of a tetradrachm, *c.* 150 B C. British Museum, London. *Photo John Webb (Brompton Studio)*

54 Bactrian silver dish showing a war-elephant, 2nd century B C. Hermitage, Leningrad. *Photo SCR*

55 Red sandstone figure of a mounted warrior, from Sarnath, 5th century A D. Sarnath Museum. *Photo courtesy the Royal Academy of Arts, London*

56 Terracotta relief of a Parthian horseman, 1st-3rd century A D. Staatliche Museen, Berlin-Dahlem

57 Stone relief of a donor couple on the south wall of the chaitya cave at Karle, 2nd century A D. *Photo Musée Guimet, Paris*

58 Model stupa from Jaulian. Archaeological Museum, Taxila

59 Sandstone figure of King Kanishka (*c.* 144-172 A D). Archaeological Museum, Mathura

60 Head of Buddha in schist, Gandhara, 3rd century A D. British Museum, London. *Photo Edwin Smith*

61 Head of Buddha in sandstone, Khmer, late 12th-early 13th century. Victoria and Albert Museum, London

62 Head of crowned Buddha in bronze, from Thailand. Staatliche Museum für Völkerkunde, Munich

63 Fragment of a relief showing Buddha enthroned, from Mathura. Staatliche Museum für Völkerkunde, Munich

64 Red sandstone railing pillar with the figure of a *yakshi*, from Kankali Tila, Mathura, 2nd century A D. State Museum, Lucknow. *Photo courtesy the Royal Academy of Arts, London*

65 Obverse of a gold coin minted by Chandra Gupta I, who came to the throne in 320 A D. British Museum, London. *Photo Ray Gardner*

66 Red sandstone lintel carved with a relief of a procession of pilgrims, from Kankali Tila, Mathura, 2nd century A D. State Museum, Lucknow

67 Remains of one of the monasteries at Nalanda. *Photo Martin Hürlimann*

68 Rama releasing Ahalya from the curse of the sage Gautama, relief of a scene from the *Ramayana*, from Deogarh, 5th century. National Museum, New Delhi

69 Iron pillar of Chandra Gupta II, Delhi, 4th-5th century. *Photo Martin Hürlimann, from his book India (London, 1967)*

70 Cast bronze statue of Buddha from Sultanganj, Bhagalpur District, first half of the 5th century. Birmingham Museum and Art Gallery

71 Hsuan-tsang's party, their path lined with priests and worshippers, enter a temple on their return to Ch'ang-an from India; section 1 of the tenth scroll of the story of the life of Hsuan-tsang. Fujita Art Museum, Osaka

72 Representation of Hsuan-tsang as a pilgrim; he carries a fly-whisk to drive away evil desires. Painting on silk from the Tun-huang caves. British Museum, London

73 'Suttee' scene, drawn by an unknown artist, *c.* 1800. India Office Library, London

74 Detail from a copy of a wall-painting in Cave 1 at Ajanta, thought to show King Pulakesin II receiving an embassy from the Persian King Chosroes II, 7th century. From John Griffiths, *The Paintings in the Buddhist Cave-temples of Ajanta*, 1896

75 Stone statue of the Bodhisattva Gautama (the future Buddha) from Sarnath in Mathura style, Kushan period (1st-3rd century A D)

76 Relief of a ship, from the Borobodur stupa, Java, 8th century.

Rijksmuseum voor Volkenkunde, Leyden

77 Detail of a limestone relief from the Amaravati stupa showing Maya's dream, c. 100 A D. British Museum, London

78 Relief showing the Buddha worshipped in a stupa, 2nd–4th century A D. Nagarjunakonda Museum. *Photo Martin Hürlimann, from his book India (London, 1967)*

79 Panoramic view of the Ajanta caves. *Photo Archaeological Survey of India, courtesy the India Office Library, London*

80 View of Badami. *Photo Richard Lannoy*

81 Kailasha temple, Ellura, dedicated by Krishna I (757–83). *Photo Victor Kennett*

82 Three-headed sculpture of Shiva Mahadeva at Elephanta, 8th–9th century. *Photo Martin Hürlimann, from his book India (London, 1967)*

83 Detail of *The Descent of the Ganges* (Arjuna's Penance), relief carved in the living rock at Mamallapuram, 7th century. *Photo Francis Watson*

84 The shore-temple, Mamallapuram, c. 700. *Photo Richard Lannoy*

85 Centre of the west front of the Borobodur stupa, Java, 8th century. *Photo Josephine Powell*

86 Bronze figure of a Chola king, from Chingleput District, Madras, 13th century. *Photo courtesy the Royal Academy of Arts, London*

87 Bronze figure of a Chola queen, from Chingleput District, Madras, 13th century. *Photo courtesy the Royal Academy of Arts, London*

88 Kutb Minar, Delhi, 12th–14th century

89 Persian wheel irrigation in the Indus valley, watercolour by Thomas Postans for his book *Personal observations in the Sindh*, published in 1843. India Office Library, London

90 Inscription on the tomb of Mahmud of Ghazni (d. 1030), Ghazni. *Photo Josephine Powell*

91 Reverse of a copper-plate land-grant from Bengal, 1196. Asutosh Museum, University of Calcutta

92 Kandariya Mahadeo temple, Khajurao, c. 1000. *Photo Barbara Wace*

93 Detail of *mithuna* couple on the Kandariya Mahadeo temple, Khajurao, c. 1000

94 Lingaraja temple, Bhuvaneshwar, 1000. *Photo Martin Hürlimann, from his book India (London, 1967)*

95 *Mithuna* couple, detail of sculpture on the east front of the Lingaraja temple, Bhuvaneshwar, c. 1000

96 Detail of *mithuna* couple on the temple of Jagannath, Puri, probably 12th century

97 Temple of Jagannath, Puri. *Photo Josephine Powell*

98 Chariot-wheel of the Sun Temple, or Black Pagoda, at Konarak, built in the reign of King Narasimha (1238–64). *Photo Francis Watson*

99 Two pages from a manuscript on palm-leaf of the *Gita Govinda* from Orissa, c. 1600. Collection Ajit Mookerjee, New Delhi. *Photo Jeff Teasdale*

100 Detail from a Persian miniature showing Chinghiz Khan. MS. Sup. Pers. 1113, fol. 99v. Bibliothèque Nationale, Paris

101 Ground floor of the Kwat-ul-Islam mosque, Delhi, begun 1193. *Photo George Mott*

102 Walls of the fort, Tughluqabad, Delhi, founded by Ghiyas-ud-din Tughluq I (reigned 1320–25). *Photo George Mott*

103 Mausoleum of Firoz Shah Tughluq (d. 1388), Delhi. *Photo Archaeological Survey of India, courtesy the India Office Library, London*

104 Mausoleum of Timur, Samarkand, early 15th century. *Photo Roger-Viollet, Paris*

105 Moghul miniature representing Timur enthroned with his descendants by Hashim, c. 1653. India Office Library, London

106 Mausoleum of Sikandar Lodi (d. 1517), Delhi. *Photo George Mott*

107 Miniature showing a Sufi, from a manuscript of Sa'di's *Bustan*, 1757. India Office Library, London

108 Moghul drawing of Kabir, c. 1700. MS. Douce Or.a.2,f.14. Courtesy the Curators of the Bodleian Library, Oxford

109 Moghul miniature showing Akbar receiving divines of various religions, by Nan Singh, from an *Akbarnama*, c. 1605. MS. 3, fol. 263b. Chester Beatty Library, Dublin

110 Portrait of Vasco da Gama, from a manuscript of Pedro Barreto de Resende's 'Account of the Viceroys of the Indies', 17th century. MS. Port. 1, fol. 13. Bibliothèque Nationale, Paris

111 Map of Portuguese Goa, from Pedro Barreto de Resende's revised edition of Antonio Bocarro's *Curo do Estado da India Oriental*, 1646. MS. Sloane 197. British Library, London

112 Moghul miniature showing Babur laying out a garden at Kabul, from a Persian translation of Babur's *Memoirs* made for Akbar in 1589. Victoria and Albert Museum, London

113 Moghul miniature showing Humayun enthroned, school of Jahangir, 1610. Freer Gallery of Art, Washington, DC

114 Detail of a Moghul miniature showing Humayun receiving his brother Kamran Mirza, c. 1590–1600. Collection of H.H. the Maharaja of Jaipur. *Photo courtesy the Royal Academy of Arts, London*

115 Humayun's library in the Purana Kila, Delhi, 16th century. *Photo George Mott*

116 Mausoleum of Humayun (d. 1555), Delhi. *Photo Victor Kennett*

117 Map of the Moghul Empire at the death of Akbar (1605). *Drawn by Hanni Bailey, after C. Collin Davies, An Historical Atlas of the Indian Peninsula (Oxford University Press, 1949)*

118 Pen sketch of Akbar, late 16th century. India Office Library, London

119 Detail of a Moghul miniature showing Adham Khan being thrown from the terrace outside the *zenana* (women's quarters)

in the palace at Agra, in 1561; from the *Akbarnama* of Abul Fazl, *c.* 1590. Victoria and Albert Museum, London

120 Detail of a Moghul miniature showing Akbar inspecting the progress of the building of Fatehpur Sikri in 1584 (near the time of its completion), from the *Akbarnama* of Abul Fazl, *c.* 1590. Victoria and Albert Museum, London

121 View of Fatehpur Sikri, looking south-west from the Panch Mahal. In the left foreground is the 'House of Miriam' – perhaps Miriam Zamani, mother of Jahangir; on the Victory Gate is inscribed, with unconscious irony: 'Jesus, on whom be peace, said, "The world is a bridge – pass over it, but build no house upon it."' *Photo Archaeological Survey of India, courtesy the India Office Library, London*

122 Moghul miniature showing Jahangir with a portrait of his father Akbar, *c.* 1599–1605. Musée Guimet, Paris. *Photo Giraudon*

123 Moghul miniature of Shah Jahan at the time of his accession in 1627. Private collection. *Photo courtesy the Royal Academy of Arts, London*

124 Taj Mahal, Agra, 1630–52. *Photo courtesy the Government of India Tourist Office, London*

125 Moghul gouache of a European traveller in India, late 16th century. Victoria and Albert Museum, London

126 Detail of a list of investors in the first voyage of the East India Company, 1599. India Office Library, London

127 View of the head office of the Dutch East India Company in Bengal, by Hendrik van Schuylenburgh, 1665. Rijksmuseum, Amsterdam

128 Portrait of Sir Thomas Roe, after Miereveldt, *c.* 1640. National Portrait Gallery, London

129 View of Aurangzeb's mosque, Banaras, watercolour by Robert Smith, 1833. India Office Library, London

130 Western Ghats landscape, water-colour by W. R. Houghton, *c.* 1878. Indian Office Library, London

131 Mughal miniature of Aurangzeb in his old age. India Office Library, London

132 Portrait of Robert Clive, by Nathaniel Dance, *c.* 1773. National Portrait Gallery, London

133 Portrait of Muhammad Ali, Nawab of the Carnatic (1717–95), by George Willison. India Office Library, London

134 Clive's agent, Watts, negotiating with Mir Jafar and his son Miran, 1757. India Office Library, London

135 Government House, Calcutta, from the east, aquatint from James Baillie Fraser's *Views of Calcutta and its Environs*, 1824–6. Private collection

136 Portrait of Warren Hastings, painted by Tilly Kettle during his stay in India (1769–76). National Portrait Gallery, London

137 The British Residency at Hyderabad in 1813, etching from Captain Robert Melville Grindlay's *Scenery, Costumes and Architecture of India*, 1826–30. India Office Library, London

138 Tipu Sultan giving his two sons as hostages to Cornwallis, medallion by C. H. Kuchler, 1792. Private collection.

139 Colonel James Skinner and one of his sons holding a regimental durbar at Hansi, watercolour by Ghulam Ali Khan, Delhi, 1827–8. National Army Museum, Camberley, Surrey

140 Ghazi-ud-din Haidar, Nawab and King of Oudh (1814–17), entertaining Lord and Lady Moira to a banquet in his palace at Lucknow in 1814, gouache by a Lucknow artist. India Office Library, London

141 A bazaar in Sindhia's camp, etching from T. D. Broughton's *Letters written in a Mahratta Camp during the year 1809*, London, 1813

142 *Bolan Pass*, watercolour by an unknown amateur artist, *c.* 1840. National Army Museum, Camberley, Surrey

143 Indian ruler in British uniform, by a Jaipur artist, *c.* 1860. Victoria and Albert Museum, London

144 Detail of a portrait of Dr George Wombwell in Indian dress, gouache by a Lucknow artist, *c.* 1780–90, perhaps after a now lost painting by Tilly Kettle of the early 1770s. Private collection

145 Portrait of Raja Ram Mohun Roy (1770–1833), by a Delhi artist. Victoria and Albert Museum, London

146 A group of Thugs in jail. India Office Library, London

147 Model in carved and painted wood of an Indian court, from Kondapalli, Andhra Pradesh, first half of the 19th century. Victoria and Albert Museum, London

148 Detail of a lithograph showing a railway train, by a Sikh artist, second half of the 19th century. Victoria and Albert Museum, London

149 'Levelling and marking out the line', lithograph from the pamphlet, *Account of the Electric Telegraph and the Railway for Children and Grown Up People in Punjaubi*, Amritsar, June 1865. Church Missionary Society, London

150 View of the Ganges Canal at Roorkee, watercolour by William Simpson, 1863. India Office Library, London

151 Sepoys at rifle practice, from Captain G. F. Atkinson's *Campaign in India 1857–8*. National Army Museum, Camberley, Surrey

152 Lithograph showing the storming of Delhi during the Indian Mutiny, 1857. *Photo Radio Times Hulton Picture Library*

153 View of Lucknow after the Mutiny, 1858: the Cawnpore Road taken from the direction of the Cawnpore Battery in the Residency. *Photo Radio Times Hulton Picture Library*

154 Queen Victoria, photographed by W. and D. Downey in 1873. The ivory throne had been shown at the Great Exhibition in London in 1851. *Photo Radio*

Times Hulton Picture Library

155 Lord Canning visiting the Maharaja of Kashmir at Sialkot, 9 March 1860, by William Simpson. India Office Library, London

156 First Indian National Congress, 1885. India Office Library, London

157 The Bala Hisar fort, photographed from the gateway above the British Residency at Kabul during the Second Afghan War, *c.* 1878. *Photo Radio Times Hulton Picture Library*

158 Baggage-train of the Younghusband expedition to Tibet, 1904. National Army Museum, Camberley, Surrey

159 Portrait of Lord Curzon, by J. Cooke after John Singer Sargent. National Portrait Gallery, London

160 Mahatma Gandhi at the session in Ahmadabad of the Indian National Congress, December 1921. India Office Library, London

161 Repression of a demonstration at Amritsar, April 1923. *Photo John Allen, New York*

162 Mahatma Gandhi on the Salt March, 1930. *Photo Radio Times Hulton Picture Library*

163 Mahatma Gandhi at the Round Table Conference, London, 1931. India Office Library, London

164 M. A. Jinnah in 1946. India Office Library, London

165 Calcutta police using tear gas during an attempt to set fire to a Hindu temple (right) during riots in August 1946. *Photo Keystone*

166 Dr Rajendra Prasad and Jawaharlal Nehru at a meeting of the Constituent Assembly in New Delhi, 1946/7. *Photo Radio Times Hulton Picture Library*

167 Mrs Indira Gandhi at the celebrations of the 25th anniversary of independence, Delhi, 1972. *Photo Associated Press*

168 Lord and Lady Mountbatten hailed by crowds in New Delhi on the first day of independence, 15 August 1947. *Photo United Press International*

169 Mahatma Gandhi lying in state, 1948. *Photo Press Information Bureau, Government of India*

170 Vallabhai Patel in 1947. *Photo Radio Times Hulton Picture Library*

171 Designs representing Indian political parties. Top row (left to right): Congress, Socialist Party, Forward Block, and Kisan Mazdoor Praja Party. Second row: Communist Party, Revolutionary Socialist Party, Krishikar Lok Party, and Jan Sangh. Third row: Forward Block, Hindu Maha Sabha, and Ram Rajya Parishad. Bottom row: Scheduled Caste Federation, Revolutionary Communist Party, and Bolshevist Party. *Photo Press Information Bureau, Government of India.*

172 View of a polling station. *Photo Press Information Bureau, Government of India*

173 Jawaharlal Nehru inaugurating a Community Development Project, the construction of a connecting road between the Grand Trunk Road and Alipur village (near Delhi), 2 October 1952. *Photo Press Information Bureau, Government of India*

174 Nochikuppam – Nochinagar slum clearance scheme, Tamil Nadu. *Photo Barbara Wace*

175 Building of the Tungabhadra dam. *Photo Richard Lannoy*

176 Labourers preparing a meal outside the Durgapur steel works in Bengal. *Photo Terry Fincher/Camera Press*

177 Class in a nursery school at Chandigarh. *Photo Delia G. Tyrwhitt/Camera Press*

178 View of the highway between Katmandu and India. *Photo A.C. Barrington Brown/Camera Press*

179 Indian scholars in Ladakh, November 1962. *Photo Keystone*

180 Jawaharlal Nehru with Marshal Bulganin in Moscow, 1955. *Photo Camera Press*

181 View of the funeral procession of Jawaharlal Nehru, New Delhi, May 1964. *Photo Camera Press*

182 Cirus, 40-megawatt experimental atomic reactor at Trombay, near Bombay. *Photo David Channer/Camera Press*

183 Congress Party poster for the March 1977 general election. *Photo Dieter Ludwig/Sipa/Rex*

184 Sanjay Gandhi's Youth Congress poster in Karnal, Haryana, for the March 1977 general election. *Photo Dieter Ludwig/Sipa/Rex*

185 Sikh rioter being arrested in Amritsar, June 1983. *Photo Dieter Ludwig/Sipa/Rex*

186 Indira Gandhi with her bodyguard Beant Singh in January 1980. *Photo Thierry Boccon-Gibod/Sipa/Rex*

187 Militant Hindus on the domes of the Babri Mosque, Ayodhya, 6 December 1992. *Photo Prashant Panjiar/Sipa/Rex*

188 Billboard advertising computer training, Bangalore, March 2000. *Photo Thomas Haley/Sipa/Rex*

Index

Numerals in *italic* type refer to illustration numbers

Abbasids 87
Abul Fazl 117
Adham Khan 112; *119*
Advaita doctrine 83
Afghanistan 125, 134, 148, 183, 184; *44*
Agni 33
Agra 100, 102, 108, 116, 122; *119, 124*
Ahmad Shah Abdali 125
Ahmadnagar 105, 115, 124
Ahmed, Fakhruddin Ali 176
Ajanta 60, 75; *74, 79*
Ajatasatru 44
Ajivikas 51
Ajmer 94, 95
Akbar 109–17, 122; *105, 109, 112, 117–122*
Ala-ud-din Khilji 96, 97, 101
Al Biruni 90–91
Albuquerque, Affonso 106–7
Alexander the Great 18, 44–7; *45, 46*
Aligarh 151
Allahabad 127, 176
All-India Muslim League 150, 151, 155, 156
al-Qaeda 183
Amaravati 73; *38, 77, 78*
Amber 113, 122
Amboyna 118
Amir Khusru 102
Amritsar 152, 181; *185*
Andhra 53, 73–6
Anga 35, 44
Arabs 87–90
Aravalli hills 12
Arthashastra 44, 47, 49, 50
Aryabharta 65
Aryans 11–12, 30–32, 88
Arya Samaj 150
Aryavarta 12, 35, 82
Asaf Jah, *see* Nizam-ul-Mulk
Ashoka 17, 19, 49–51, 53, 61, 67, 71; *2, 9, 49, 50, 51*
Assam 179
Atreya 35

Attlee, Clement 156
Auckland, Lord 134
Aurangzeb 17, 121–4; *129, 131*
Australia 171
Ayodhya 63, 182; *187*

Babur 100, 101, 108–9, 182; *105, 112*
Bactria 53–6, 59
Badami 76; *80*
Baghdad 87, 96
Bahadur Shah I 124
Bahadur Shah II 143
Bahmani state 98, 105
Baigas 21
Bairam Khan 112
Baji Rao I 124
Balban 96
Bali 83
Baluchistan 21, 115
Banaras (Varanasi) 35, 41, 56, 90, 95, 102, 121; *43, 129*
Banerji, R. D. 19
Bangladesh 176
Barabar caves 51; *51*
Barna 68
Barygaza (Broach) 72
Begram 59
Bengal 35, 69, 72, 78, 87, 94, 95, 98, 102, 105, 112, 115, 121, 124, 125, 127, 150–51, 159, 176
Bengal Army 140–41, 147
Berar 76, 105, 115
Besant, Annie 150
Besnagar 55
Bhagavad-Gita 18, 37
Bhagwan Das 113
bhakti movement 94, 102
Bharata Natyam 85
Bharatya Janata Party (BJP) 182
Bhonsla 129, 131
Bhutan 171
Bhuvaneshwar 91; *94, 95*
Bidar 105
Bihar 35, 39, 51, 95, 112, 127, 168; *9, 40*

Bijapur 105, 106, 122
Bimbisara 44
Bindusura 47
bin Laden, Osama 183, 184
Bodh-Gaya 41; *41*
Bolan pass 12; *142*
Bombay (Mumbai) 55, 120, 125, 130, 136, 140, 146, 147, 169, 179
Borobodur 84; *76, 85*
Bose, Subhas Chandra 148
Brahma 33; *32, 65*
Brahmagupta 68
Brahmanabad 87
Brahmanas 37
Brahmanism 39, 51, 53, 54, 60, 62, 81, 82, 83–4
brahmans, *see* caste
Brahmaputra 12
Brahmi 19
Brahui 21
Brezhnev, Leonid 175
Broach 72
Buddha 33, 39, 40–43, 50; *38–43, 60–62, 65, 70*
Buddhism 39–43, 50, 51, 56–7, 59, 61–2, 69, 81, 83–4, 90, 180
Bulganin, Marshal Nikolai *180*
Bundelkhand 91
Burgess, James 19
Burke, Edmund *129, 137*
Burma 11, 14–15, 57, 133, 148, 159
Burnouf, Eugène 19
Bush, George W. 183
Buxar 127

Calcutta 121, 125, 127, 128, 136, 141, 145, 146; *12, 127, 135, 165*
    Black Hole of 126
Calcutta Council 126, 127
Calicut 105
Cambodia 72, 83
Canada 171, 176
Canning, Charles John, Lord 145, 146; *155*
Cardamom hills 14; *7*

Carey, William 137
Carnatic, nawabs of the 125, 126; *133*
caste 31, 50, 68, 85, 87, 90, 122, 181, 184; *31*
Catherine of Braganza 120
Cautley, Sir P. T. *150*
Cawnpore (Kanpur) 141, 144
Celebes 73
Ceylon (Sri Lanka) 14, 51, 57, 84, 120, 131, 159
Chaitanya 102
Chalukyas 76, 80, 87; *80*
Champa 83, 84
Chandernagar 125, 126, 161
Chandidas 102
Chandigarh 177
Chandra Gupta I 61
Chandra Gupta II 63, 64; *69*
Chandragupta Maurya 44, 46–7, 49, 50, 54
Chanhu-Daro 27; *23*
Charles II, King of England 120
Chauhans 94
Cheras 82
China 11, 164, 171–3, 175, 181, 182, 184
Chinghiz Khan 95–6, 108; *100*
Chitor 96, 113
Chola dynasty 72, 80, 84–5; *86, 87*
Clinton, Bill 183
Clive, Robert, Lord 125–9; *132*
Cloud Messenger 63
Cochin 106
Colombo 120
Colombo Plan 170–71; *178*
Commonwealth, British 176, 180
Communist Party of India 164, 173, 175; *171*
Communist Party of India (Marxist) 175
Compagnie des Indes 126
Congress Party and Indian National Congress 147, 150–57, 162, 164, 175, 176, 178, 181; *156, 163, 171, 183, 184*
Conjeevaram 81
Conti, Nicolo 105
Coote, Eyre 127
Cornwallis, Lord 85, 130, 135; *138*
Cotton, Henry 147
Cranganore 72
Cripps, Sir Stafford 152, 155
Cunningham, Alexander 19
Curzon, George Nathaniel, Lord 19, 146, 148, 150; *159*

Cyrus 35

Dalhousie, Lord 134, 139–40
Dandin 76
Darius 35
Daulatabad 98
Dayanand, Swami 150
de Bussy, Marquis 126
Deccan 14, 53, 61, 71ff., 96, 124, 131
Dehra Dun 148
Delhi 35, 64, 95, 97, 98, 100, 108, 109, 118, 123, 124, 132, 140, 141, 143, 145, 154, 157, 159, 181; *88, 101–103, 106, 115, 116, 152, 167–169, 181*
Denmark 120, 137
Deogiri 98
Desai, Morarji 175, 179
Deve Gowda, H. D. 182
Din-i-Illai 116
Diu 107
Diwani 127
Dravidians 31, 82, 85
Dufferin, Lord 147
Duperron, A. H. Anquetil- 36
Dupleix, Joseph François 125, 126
Durgapur *173*
Dutch, *see* Holland
Dyauspitar 33
Dyer, General Reginald 152

East India Company 19, 119, 120–21, 124–7, 129–30; *126, 147*
Egypt 175
Elephanta 78; *82*
Elizabeth I, Queen of England 119
Ellenborough, Lord 134
Ellura 75, 78; *81, 82*
Elphinstone, Mountstuart 132, 140
Emergency, State of 176, 178, 184
England 119–21, 125–7, 129ff.
Ephthalites 66
Eucratides *54*

Fa-hsien 60, 67
Fatehpur Sikri 115–16; *120, 121*
Firdausi 90
Firoz Shah Tughluq 98, 101; *88, 103*
Fitch, Ralph *120*
Five Year Plans 164, 166, 168, 170

Fort St George 125
Fort William 121, 124, 126
France 120, 125–6, 127, 182
Francis Xavier, St 108
Fu-nan 72, 80, 83

Gaikwar 129, 133
Gandhara 35, 45, 47, 53, 54, 56–9, 61, 73; *60*
Ghandhi, Indira 175, 176, 178, 179, 181; *167, 182, 183, 186*
Gandhi, Mahatma 151, 152, 154, 155–7, 159, 162, 163–4, 171; *160–163, 169*
Gandhi, Rajiv 179, 181
Gandhi, Sanjay 178, 179; *184*
Ganesha 34, 151; *34*
Ganga dynasty 91
Ganges 34–5, 39, 47, 56, 61, 96
Garuda column 55
Garwhal 133
Gautama 39, 40–43, 50; *see also* Buddha
Genghiz Khan, *see* Chinghiz Khan
George V, King of England 145
George VI, King of England 157
Germany, West 166
Ghazi-ud-din Haidar, Nawab and King of Oudh *140*
Ghaznavids 89–90
Ghazni *90*
Ghiyas-ud-din Tughluq 98; *102*
Ghosh, Aurobindo 151
Girnar 49
Gita Govinda 94; *99*
Goa 84, 106, 108, 161; *111*
Godavari river 14, 73
Gokhale, G. K. 151
Golconda 105, 122
Gomal pass 12
Gondopharnes 56
Gonds 21; *17*
Govinda III 78
Great Britain *182*; *see also* England
Greeks 44–7, 53–6
Green Revolution 183
Gujaral, I. K. 182
Gujarat 40, 87, 98, 115, 124, 179, 184
Gumti river 98
Gupta dynasty 60–65; *67–70*
Gurjara-Pratiharas 87
Gurjaras 76
Gurkhas 133, 148
Gwalior 95

Haidar Ali 130
Han dynasty 56
Hansi *139*
Hanuman 34; *35*
Harappa 23, 27, 30; *23, 25, 26, 29*
Hariyupiya 30
Harsha Vardhana 66–9, 76
Haryana 180
Hastinaputra 35
Hastings, Lord, *see* Moira
Hastings, Warren 18, 127,
    129–31, 135, 136; *136*
Hawkins, William 120
Heliodorus 55
Herodotus 45
Himalayas 11, 148; *3*
Himu 112
Hinayana Buddhism 57, 81
Hinduism and Hindus 15, 33ff.,
    72, 82, 84, 85, 87, 89, 90,
    91–2, 94, 98, 100, 102, 105–6,
    108, 112–17, 121–3, 126,
    134–5, 137–8, 139, 141, 150,
    155, 159–62, 180, 181, 182,
    184; *187; see also* Brahmanism,
    and the names of the deities
Hindu Kush 11, 45; *44*
Hindustan 12, 89
Hodgson, Brian 19
Holkar 129, 131, 133
Holland 119–21, 131; *127*
Horse Sacrifice, Great 53, 60
Hoysalas 85
Hsuan-tsang 15, 56, 67, 68, 76; *71,
    72*
Hulagu 96, 102
Humayun 108–9, 116; *105,
    113–115*
Hume, Allan Octavian 147
Huns, 60, 62, 66, 76, 88
Hyderabad 126, 161; *137*

Ibn Batuta 98
Ibrahim Lodi 105, 108
Ilbert Bill 146, 147
Iltutmish 95
India Act (1784) 131, 135
Indian Civil Service 146, 147
Indian Council Act (1892) 151
Indian National Congress, *see*
    Congress
Indra 30, 33
Indraprastha 35
Irwin, Lord 152
Islam, *see* Muslims
Israel 182

Jahangir 113, 116, 117, 120; *11,
    105, 122*

Jainism 39–40, 51, 78, 81, 90
Jaipur 113
Janata party 178, 179; *183*
Japan 148, 156
Jaunpur 98
Java 83, 84
Jayadeva 94, 102
Jinnah, Muhammad Ali 155,
    156, 164; *164*
jizya tax 101, 113
Jones, Sir William 18
Jumna river 34, 96
Junagadh 73

Kabir 102; *108*
Kabul 46, 108, 124; *112, 157*
Kalhana 19
Kali 151
Kalidasa 60, 63
Kalingas 50, 53
Kamarupa 61
Kama Sutra 63–4
Kamran *114*
Kanauj 66, 69, 78, 89
Kanchi 81, 82
Kanishka 56; *59*
Kanpur, *see* Cawnpore
Kanua 108
Kapilavastu 40
Karle 55, 75; *55*
karma 39, 55
Karnal *184*
Kashgar 56
Kashmir 19, 36, 56, 61, 87, 115,
    134, 161, 173, 183, 184–5
Kathiawar 53
Kauravas 34
Kaushala 44
Kaushambi 35
Kautilya 44
Kaveri river *6*
Kazakhstan 181
Kerala 82
Kettle, Tilly *136*
Khajurao 91; *92, 93*
Khalistan 181
Khan, Liaqat Ali 164
Khan, Syed Ahmad 151
Khilji Sultans 96, 97, 101
Khotan 56
Khyber pass 12, 134, 148
Kistna river, *see* Krishna river
Kolis 21; *16*
Konarak 91; *98*
Kosala 36
Kosambi, D. D. 23
Krishna 33, 34, 37, 60, 85, 94; *99*
Krishna I 78
Krishna (Kistna) river 14, 73

Krishnadeva Raya 108
kshatriyas, *see* caste
Kublai Khan 85
Kumaon 61, 133
Kushan dynasty 56–60
Kutb Minar, *95; 88*
Kutb-ud-din Aibak 95; *88*
Kwat-ul-Islam mosque 95; *101*

Laccadive islands 84
Ladakh 161, 172, 173; *179*
Lahore 89
Lake, General Gerard 131, 132
Lauriya Nandangarh *50*
Lawrence, Henry 134, 141
Lawrence, John 134, 141
Laws of Manu 65, 68
Lhasa 148, 172
Lichchavi 60
Linlithgow, Lord 155
Lodi kings 100–101, 105, 108;
    103, 106
Lomas Rishi cave *51*
Lucknow 141, 143; *140, 153*

Macaulay, T. B. 137, 146
Mackenzie, Colin 19; *13*
Madras (Chenai) 56, 73, 120,
    125, 126, 130, 136, 146, 147,
    181
Madurai 72, 85, 96
Magadha 35, 36, 43–4, 46, 47,
    53, 61
Mahabharata 34, 35, 37, 63, 102
Maharashtra 102, 129, 140, 179
Mahavira 39
Mahayana Buddhism 57, 83
Mahendravarman I 81
Mahmud of Ghazni 89–90, 94;
    90
Majapahit 84
Malabar 87, 105
Malacca 107
Malaya 84
Malay peninsula 72, 83
Malcolm, Sir John 132, 136
Maldive islands 84
Mallas 39
Malwa 95, 98, 113, 124
Mamallapuram 81, 82; *83, 84*
Manu, Laws of 65, 68
Maratha Confederacy 130, 131
Marathas 122–3, 124, 125, 129
Marshall, Sir John 19
Marwar 122
Masulipatam 118
Mathura 54, 59, 73, 89, 124–5;
    59, 63, 64
Mauryan Empire 17, 47–51, 53

maya 55
Meerut 141
Megasthenes 47
Menander 53, 55; *53*
Metcalfe, Sir Charles 132
Mewar 105
Mirabai, Princess 102
Mir Jafar 127; *134*
Mir Kasim 127
Mithridates 54
Mizo 21
Moghuls 108ff., 125; *105, 109,
    112–124, 131*
Mohenjo-Daro 23, 26, 27, 30, 31;
    8, 20–23, 24, 27–29
Moira, Earl of (Marquess of
    Hastings) 132, 133, 140; *140*
Mongols 95–7
Montagu–Chelmsford Reforms
    152
Morley–Minto Reforms 151
Mountbatten, Lord 157; *168*
Muhammad Ali, Nawab of
    Carnatic 126, *133*
Muhammad bin Tughluq 97–8,
    124
Muhammad Ghuri 90, 95
Muhammad Shah 124
Müller, Max 33
Mumtaz 117
Munro, Hector 127
Munro, Sir Thomas 132, 136
Musharraf, Pervez 184–5
Musiris 72
Muslim League 150, 151, 155,
    156
Muslims 90, 92, 95, 100–102,
    105, 113, 115–17, 122, 123,
    135, 136, 141, 150–51, 154–6,
    159–62, 182, 183, 184, 185;
    187
Mutiny 140–43, 145, 147; *152,
    153*
Mysore 131; *10*

Nadir Shah 124
Nagarjuna 73
Nagarjunakonda 73; *78*
nagas 35
Nagas 21, 161; *15*
Nagasena 53
Nalanda 62, 68; *67*
Nanak, Guru 102
Nana Saheb 144
Nanda dynasty 44, 46–7
Nandi *10*
Napier, Sir Charles 134
Narasimha 91
Narbada river 14, 98

Narsimha Rao, P. V. 181
Nasik 55, 76
National Democratic Alliance
    (NDA) 182
National Front 181
Naxalites 176
Nehru, Jawaharlal 15, 152, 155,
    157, 161–4, 166, 169, 171–2,
    175, 179, 181, 183; *166, 173,
    180, 181, 182, 183*
Nepal 51, 61, 133, 148, 171, 175
Nero 71
New Delhi, *see* Delhi
New Zealand 171
Nilgiri hills 14, 21; *18*
Nixon, Richard 180
Nizam-ul-Mulk 124, 126
Non-Aligned Movement 175,
    181
Nur Jahan 117

Orissa 50, 54, 83, 84, 91, 124; *94,
    95*
Ormuz 107
Oudh 63, 124, 127, 129, 135; *140*

Pakistan 11, 155, 156, 159, 161,
    173, 175, 176, 180, 182, 183,
    184–5
Palas 69, 78, 88, 94
Palembang 84
Pali 44
Pallavas 76, 80–81, 84
Panchalas 39
Pandavas 34
Pandyas 85
Panikkar, K. M. 154
Panipat 94, 112, 125
pardah 102
Parsis (Zoroastrians) 39, 87
Parthians 54; *56*
Pataliputra 47, 54; *47, 48*
Patel, Vallabhai 157, 161, 163,
    164; *170*
Pathans 148
Patna 47
Periplus of the Erythrean Sea 71, 72
Peshawar 56
Peshwa 129, 130
Pindaris 133
Pitt, William, the younger 131
Plassey 126–7
Plato 55
Pliny 71
Polo, Marco 85
Polygars 123
Pondicherry 120, 161
Poona (Pune) 124
Portugal 105–8, 118, 120, 161

Porus 46, 47; *46*
Postans, Thomas *49*
Prakrit 76
Prasad, Rajendra 157; *166*
Pratiharas 78, 87
Prinsep, James 19, 55; *14, 49*
Prithviraj III 94–5
Pulakesin II 76; *74*
Punjab 53, 89, 95, 98, 123–5,
    134, 152, 155, 159, 175, 179,
    180
Purana Qila, Delhi 109; *115*
Puranas 63
Puri 91; *96, 97*
Purna Swaraj 152
Purushapura 56

Radha *99*
Raja Bhoja 91
Rajagriha 43, 44, 47, 62
Rajaraja I 84, 85
Rajasthan 27, 102, 176
Rajendra I 84
Rajgir 43
Rajputana 114
Rajputs 76, 78, 87, 88, 90ff., 98,
    108, 113
Rama 33, 35, 182
Ramakrishna 150
Ramananda 102
Ramanuja 85, 102
Ramayana 34, 35, 63, 102; *35, 36,
    68*
Ram Mohun Roy 137, 139; *145*
Rana Sangram Singh 108
Rangoon 144
Ranjit Singh 133, 134
Ranthambor 113
Rao II 131
Rashtrakutas 76, 78, 82, 88
Ravana 35
Rig-Veda 30, 32, 36
Ripon, Lord 146
rishis 36–7; *37*
Roe, Sir Thomas 120; *128*
Rohilla 129
Romans 71–2
Round Table Conference, 1931
    152–4; *163*
Rowland, Benjamin 82
Rudra 33
Rudradaman 73
Russia 148, 156, 164, 166, 171,
    182; *see also* Soviet Union

Safavid Shah 109
Sakuntala 18, 63
Salt March 152; *162*
Samarkand 98, 108; *104*

Samudra Gupta 61
Sanchi 51, 73; *40, 52*
Sanskrit 18, 31, 32, 35, 84
San Thome 120
Sarnath 41; *43, 55*
Satavahana dynasty 73–6
sati, see suttee
Satpura line 14
Saurashtra 53, 73, 89
Sayyids 100
Schopenhauer, Arthur 36
Scythians 53–4
Seeley, Sir J. R. 18
Seleucus Nikator 47
Sena dynasty 94
Serampore 137
Seringapatam 130
Shah Alam II 127, 129
Shah Jahan 117, 120, 122; *123, 124*
Shahjahanabad (Delhi) 118
Shaik Salim Chisti *121*
Shailendras 83, 84
Shaivites 83, 85
Shakas 54, 56, 73
Shankara 82, 85
Shankaracharya 82
Sharif, Nawaz 183
Shastri, Lal Bahadur 163, 175
Shekhar, Chandra 181
Sher Shah 109; *115*
Shias 100
Shiva 26, 33, 37, 81, 83, 85, 94, 151; *33*
Shivaji 122, 123, 151
Shivalingam 81
Shrivijaya 84
shudras, *see* caste
Shunga dynasty 53
Sialkot 53
Sikandar Lodi *103, 106*
Sikhs 123, 159, 163, 181; *148, 185, 186*
Sikh Wars 134
Sikkim 171
Sind 78, 87, 94, 115, 124, 134, 148
Sindhia 129, 130, 131, 132, 133; *141*
Singh, Beant *186*
Singh, Vishwanath Pratap 181
Singh, Zail 181
Siraj-ud-daula 124, 126
Sirsukh 56–7
Sita 35
Skanda Gupta 66
Skinner, Colonel James 132; *139*
Slave dynasty 95, 96
Sleeman, William 138

Somnath 89
Soviet Union 175, 180, 181, 183
Spear, Sir Percival 135
Sri Lanka 14, 159, 180, 181; *see also* Ceylon
States Reorganization Commission 163
Suez Canal 147
Sufism 102; *107*
Sultanganj *70*
Sumatra 83, 84
Sunnis 100
Surat 118, 120, 121, 122
Surdas 102
Surya 33, 91
Susruta 68
suttee (*sati*) 68, 138; *73*

Taj Mahal 117, 118
Taliban 184
Talikota 115
Tamerlaine, *see* Timur
Tamils 180, 181
Tanjore 84, 85, 122
Tantrism 94
Tapti river 98
Taraori 94
Tarapur 176
Tashkent 175
Taxila 35, 46, 47, 50, 53, 56; *58*
Tegh Bahadur 123
Thailand 57; *62*
Thanesar 66
Thar desert 12
Thomas, 'King' 132
Thomas, St 56
Thugs 138; *146*
Tiberius 71
Tibet 148, 171
Tilak, B. G. 151
Timur 98–9, 105, 108; *104, 105*
Tipu Sultan 130; *138*
Todar Mall 114
Todas 21; *18*
Tranquebar 120
Trombay *182*
Tughluqabad *102*
Tughluq dynasty 17, 97–8, 100, 101; *102*
Tungabhadra river 14, 85; dam 175

Ujjain 50, 54, 63, 66
Ulema 100, 116
Umayyads 87
United East India Company 119
United Front 182

United Nations 171, 175, 185
United States 180, 181, 182, 183, 184–5
Upanishads 36–7
Urdu 102
Usha 33
Uzbekistan 175

Vaisesika 68
Vaishnavite 94
vaishyas, *see* caste
Vajpayee, Atal Behari 182
Vakatakas 76
Valmiki 34
Varanasi, *see* Banaras
Varuna 33
Vasco da Gama 105–6; *110*
Vasudeva 60
Vatsyayana 63
Vedanta 82
Vedas 30–31
Victoria, Queen of England 144–5; *154*
Videhas 39
Vidyapati 102
Vietnam 84
Vijayanagar 85, 98, 105, 108, 115, 120
Vindhya hills 14, 35
Vishnu 33, 62, 78, 85; *91*
Vishnu-Jaganath 91
Vivekananda, Swami 150

Watson, Admiral Charles 126
Wavell, Lord 156
Wedderburn, William 147
Wellesley, Lord 130–32; *135*
Wellington, Duke of, 130, 131
Western Ghats 14, 76; *130*
Wheeler, Sir Mortimer 30, 31
Wilkins, C. H. 18
Woodruff, Philip 147
World Bank 161
World Hindu Council 181
World Trade Organization 185

Yama 33
Yarkand 56
Yasodharman 66
Yasovarman I 81
Yavanas 54
yogi 37
Younghusband Expedition 148; *158*
Yugoslavia 175
Yule, David 147

Zamorin 105–6
Zoroastrians, *see* Parsis